HE DID HIS BIT

The Stories behind the Shirt Collection
of Welsh Rugby Legend

CHARLIE PRITCHARD

PETER JONES

Gomer

First published in 2020 by Gomer Press,
Llandysul, Ceredigion SA44 4JL

ISBN 978 1 78562 315 8

A CIP record for this title is available from the British Library.

© Text copyright Peter Jones, 2020
© Photography copyright Emyr Young, 2020

Peter Jones asserts his moral right under the
Copyright, Designs and Patents Act, 1988
to be identified as author of this work.

This book is published with the financial support of the
Books Council of Wales.

Printed and bound in Wales at
Gomer Press, Llandysul, Ceredigion
www.gomer.co.uk

To Coralie

'What will survive of us is love …'

The first team to beat the New Zealanders: The Victorious Wales XV

FOREWORD

By Phil McGowan (Museum Curator, World Rugby Museum)

When most people consider the history of Welsh rugby it is players such as Gareth Edwards, Phil Bennett, Gerald Davies and JPR Williams who dart into view, usually with a handful of English, Scottish or French pursuers trailing desperately in their wake.

Rugby historians like Peter Jones, however, are duty bound to see the bigger picture. British Pathé film men were there in the 1950s when Cliff Morgan's trickery and guile inspired an earlier generation of Welsh rugby fans. Earlier still we are reliant on the match reports and eulogies of those who bore witness to the *first* golden age of Welsh rugby.

Perhaps it is when reading the accounts of the likes of correspondent WJT Collins ('Dromio') and his depictions of *'the greatest rugby player of all time'* Arthur 'Monkey' Gould that the thought first occurs – maybe that seventies team wasn't the greatest after all?

Six outright Welsh championships were secured in the eleven years between 1969 and 1979. Six were also secured in the eleven years between 1900 and 1911. The 1970s vintage boasts three Grand Slams in 1971, 1976 and 1978. Victories over the French in 1908 and 1909 and a slam in 1911 mean that the earlier side can boast the same.

What separates the two sides is the small matter of a game played on a cold winter's day at Cardiff Arms Park on 16 December 1905. A touring New Zealand side, newly nicknamed the 'All Blacks', had comfortably beaten every side put in front of them in the two months leading up to their very first game on Welsh soil.

Despite being almost unknown when they arrived, Test match victories against Scotland, Ireland and England had gone so far as to create an air of invincibility around the men in black. But a Welsh team that featured Gwyn Nicholls, Rhys Gabe, Teddy Morgan and Bert Winfield would not likely be overawed. Having secured a dominant clean sweep of the Home Nations Championship earlier in the year, Wales would condemn the visitors to the first and only defeat of the tour. It was a narrow victory but one that established Wales, at that moment in time, as indisputably the world's best rugby team.

The newspaper reports that followed singled out one individual as the difference between the two sides – the Newport forward Charlie Pritchard.

This publication, by Peter Jones, brings clarity to the experiences of a man who stood out on one of the world's greatest sporting stages. A decade later he would do the same on the field of battle. His is a name that should be remembered by rugby fans of every stripe around the world and Peter's book will ensure he is.

ACKNOWLEDGEMENTS

A couple of years ago I was lucky enough to work on a book called *Newport Rugby Greats*. It was a hugely enjoyable project, about one of the sport's most famous clubs. It is impossible to visit Rodney Parade without some of the history of the place seeping into your bones. In talking to some 'greats' – Bryn Meredith, Brian Price, Keith Jarrett, David Watkins, Dick Uzzell and Brian Jones from the fifties and sixties to more recent players such as Paul Turner and Jason Forster – I was struck by their sense of being a part of something beyond their own careers. They all felt proud to be part of the Rodney Parade story.

When I delved further back into the stories of some past wearers of the famous old Black and Amber jersey, the pride of living relatives shone through too. This was particularly the case with Mr and Mrs Douglas-Phillips. Geraldine Douglas-Phillips is the grand daughter of Charlie Pritchard, the athletic and brave forward who graced Rodney Parade in the early part of the twentieth century. He lost his life in World War 1, and Geraldine is the daughter of the little girl who was born four months or so after her father had been killed. A picture of Charlie now sits in front of the TV on match days at their little cottage near Winchester in Hampshire. There is no exile like a Welsh exile, as my own family can attest.

Soon I had met Gareth Pritchard, Charlie's great grandson, at his home in Dorset. Gareth brought a sizeable plastic box down from his attic and unpacked Charlie's shirt collection and the project took off. For a rugby-mad World War 1 geek, it was difficult to imagine not getting involved. My heartfelt thanks to the whole Pritchard clan – past, present and future. I hope that I have done you proud.

My thanks also to Phil McGowan and his team at the Twickenham World Rugby Museum. His expertise and enthusiasm for the project has been a source of constant support. I know I speak for the family when I say that they are all proud that this precious collection of shirts is now being shared with rugby fans, helping us all to learn more about the game we love.

All the shirts in the collection tell a story, and I have enjoyed reading (and re-reading) some excellent rugby writing as I worked on the background to each one. The work of Gwyn Prescott (*Call Them to Remembrance – The Welsh rugby internationals who died in the Great War*), Huw Richards (*A Game for Hooligans*) and Stephen Cooper (*The Final Whistle: The Great War in Fifteen Players*) were a great starting point. The impressive history of Welsh rugby by David Smith and Gareth Williams, *Fields of Praise,* remains an indispensable piece of work for anyone wishing to try to understand the enormity of the social, economic and political forces at work as the game developed in Wales. David Parry-Jones' highly readable *Prince Gwyn: Gwyn Nicholls and the First Golden Era of Welsh Rugby* offered a superb insight into the period.

There was reference support from another great journalist, John Billot, whose *History of Welsh Rugby Internationals* was beside me most of the way. Likewise, the tab for the excellent website at www.blackandambers.co.uk stayed open throughout.

Diolch yn fawr to Susan Roberts and the team at Gomer Press for all their work in bringing this project to fruition, and to photographer Emyr Young.

Last but not least, my thanks must also go to Kevin Jarvis, Stephen Bennett and the folk at the Friends of Newport Rugby, whose enthusiasm for their club is infectious. When I worked on *Newport Rugby Greats* I was welcomed into the Rodney Parade family, and this book would not have been written without you all. The world rugby family is huge, and I hope this book has a little something for fans from both hemispheres, but I take great pride in writing about one of Newport RFC's greatest players. Rodney Parade is one of rugby union's spiritual homes, and Charlie's shirt collection shows how some of the world's greatest players all played a part in its story. C'mon the Port!

PICTURE ACKNOWLEDEMENTS:
The Pritchard Family: Pgs xi, 3, 4, 6
World Rugby Museum, Twickenham: Pgs xii, 28, 42, 89, 141, 162, 184, 191
Newport RFC Archives: Pgs 44, 156, 161, 168
Willow Murray: Pg 107
Frederic Humbert: Pgs 135, 137
The Royal Welsh Military Museum, Brecon: 170

CONTENTS

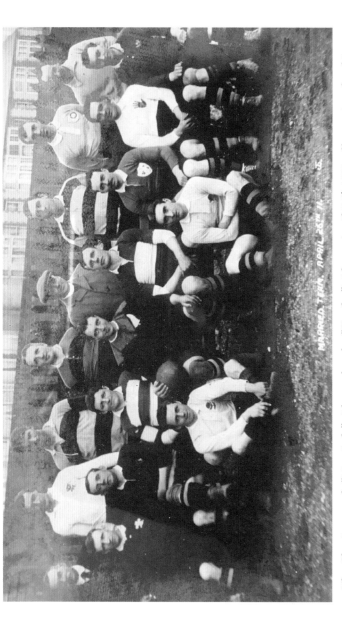

The Charity match "Marrieds" side to play the "Singles" side on April 26th 1911, all sporting the shirts from Charlie's collection. The players and shirts are as follows:

Back row, left to right: Harry Uzzell (England), Ben Uzzell (Newport), Charlie Hews (Newport), Percy Jones (Cardiff), George Travers (France)

Middle Row: Dai Boots (Wales), JJ Hodges (South Africa), Beddoe Thomas (Watsonians), CM Pritchard (NZ), George Boots (Anglo-Welsh), WJ Winfield (South Africa), H. Wreford (Ulster)

Front row, half backs: H Jones (New South Wales), Fred Birt (Australia)

THE USKSIDE APOLLO

'I grew up among heroes who went down the pit, who played rugby, told stories, sang songs of war.'

Richard Burton

His face was waxen, his life draining away. Charlie Pritchard opened his eyes one last time and spoke in an urgent whisper.

'Have they got the Hun?'

'Yes, Pritch. He is in all right,' came the reply.

'Well,' said Pritchard. 'I have done my bit.'

He slipped away during the night of 14 August 1916, seemingly resigned to his fate, and comforted by the news that the German prisoner he had captured on the trench raid was safely in custody.

Captain Charles Meyrick Pritchard had stood up to the ultimate challenge of leading men at the front, but he is remembered most as an exceptional rugby player in what was an exceptional team. Charlie played for Wales during their 'golden age' at the start of the twentieth century. He was considered by some observers to be the Man of the Match in what has become known as one of the most famous rugby matches of all time – the Welsh victory over the rampant All Black touring side of 1905. Although his playing days were over by the time war was declared, the loss of such a figure would be felt wherever people played the game, and particularly in his home town of Newport.

In the family home on Llwynderi Road, Newport, his pregnant wife Florence was left having to explain the inexplicable to Cliff and Mick, their two young sons. The eldest, the twelve-year-old Cliff, went off into the fields where his father used to teach him to shoot rabbits. A short while later, a dead rabbit lay on the family kitchen table. 'That's for Dad,' said the boy.

A century later, Charlie's shirt collection is on display at the World Rugby Museum in Twickenham. It is typical of the man that he should use these famous shirts to raise money for local worthy causes. His rugby pals would be invited to don the shirts and play in charity matches at Rodney Parade, Newport RFC's ground. For Charlie, each shirt told a story of a particular match, or of a specific opponent. This book aims to tell Charlie's rugby story through his collection. Given that his career spanned a time of rapid development in the sport, Charlie's shirts give us a unique insight into that period. For the Welsh rugby fan, the collection throws some light on a golden age at the beginning of the twentieth century, when Pritchard was at the heart of a truly great side. This collection, however, takes us far beyond the boundaries of Wales. The shirts of England, Ireland, Scotland and France are also represented. There is also an Anglo-Welsh touring shirt from an early version of a Lions tour in 1908. Charlie also managed to obtain shirts from the very first European touring sides from the southern hemisphere giants – New Zealand, Australia and South Africa. His six years in international rugby from 1904 to 1910 saw the game going global. The Pritchard Collection has something for all rugby fans because Charlie's story is the story of the game itself.

Charlie Pritchard was born in Newport in 1882 into a sporting family. His brothers Ivan and Percy also played for Newport RFC. His father, John Pritchard, was a founding member of the Newport Athletic Club. A wicketkeeper of some renown, he had once been offered a chance to play for an 'All England' side by EM Grace, the brother of that famous Victorian icon, WG Grace. The young Charlie played some cricket, but his schooling at Newport Intermediate meant that he was playing soccer in the winter months. A move to a rugby-playing school at Long Ashton in Bristol decided his fate. After school, the move into the family wine business and a black and amber Newport rugby shirt was inevitable.

There is an early pen portrait of the emerging Welsh rugby star in

EHD Sewell's *Rugby Chat* that gives us an insight into the affection in which Charlie was held.

'Known as "Goo-Goo" to his intimates, Pritchard, who is a married man with two sturdy sons, is something of a master in the art of horticulture. Winter and summer he may be seen wearing a result of his labours in this delightful hobby. Shooting and fishing he delights in, and has also wielded the willow …'

The family story is that the nick name of 'Goo-Goo' originated from his early years, when his wide eyed responses were characterised as 'Goo-Goo Eyes'. There is a consistent picture that emerges from various sources. Charlie was much respected and much loved. The news of his death in 1916 would have been felt keenly, even at a time when casualty lists in newspapers seemed endless. A picture of him with Cliff in the conservatory of the family home shows him as a settled family man, a keen gardener surrounded by blooms that look prolific even in a faded sepia-tinted shot.

On the rugby field, however, Charlie was a different beast.

Charlie with his son Cliff at the conservatory of the family home in Newport

Although he was imbued by a genuine spirit of sportsmanship, he was relentless and brave, the kind of player you would want on your side. Being known as 'Goo-Goo' and turning up to games with flowers in his lapel, Charlie was hardly the stereotypical Welsh 'Rhondda forward'. A look at the line-up of his fellow Welsh forwards from that era and one is reminded of the comment on a recent Munster pack: 'Mothers keep their photo on the mantelpiece to stop the kids from going too near the fire'. Charlie was the exception. At a hair's breadth under six feet tall, weighing in at thirteen stone, he was blessed with film star looks. His powerful physique would not look out of place in a modern, professional squad. Percy Bush, the impish Cardiff fly-half, dubbed him the 'Uskside Apollo'. Charlie had the necessary weight and power to make an impact in the set piece. From his early days at Rodney Parade, he had also established a reputation as a fearsome tackler. After his promotion to the senior side at Rodney Parade, his elevation to the Welsh team soon followed.

Alongside the rapid expansion of the game domestically, the last years of the nineteenth century and the start of the twentieth were punctuated by rugby tours, home and away. The Pritchard Collection includes the shirts of the first ever touring sides to come to Britain. The All Blacks of 1905 have gone down in New Zealand rugby history as the 'Originals', and their impact upon the game was seismic, but the Springboks of 1906 and the Wallabies of 1908 deserve recognition too. Indeed, their very names originated on those tours as the British press demanded a nickname for these exotic sporting visitors to our shores. The men who wore these three shirts from Charlie's collections were all Originals, and their tours to these shores were crucial moments in the history of the game.

Since the arrival on these shores of Dave Gallaher's Originals, the All Blacks of 1905, rugby memorabilia has become big business, but for Charlie Pritchard it was a means to a philanthropic end. He knew that in rugby-mad Newport famous players turning out in a variety of famous shirts would draw a crowd. And that crowd's gate receipts could fix a roof at a local church, or raise funds for the local rowing club. On his death in 1916, Charlie was lauded as an example of the

very best Britain could send onto the battlefield. His shirt collection is perhaps an example of the very best sport has to offer.

The Pritchard Collection gives us a unique perspective on Charlie's career, from the battered black and amber of Newport through the proud red of Wales and the iconic black of New Zealand. In some cases, we can say with some certainty who was wearing those shirts on a given match day. We know, for instance, that the Taranaki banker Frank Glasgow was wearing the All Black 7 shirt in THAT match in 1905. The Irish shirt in the collection has the name of Alfred Tedford written onto the collar, and the Irish Rugby Union were prescient enough to add the '1906' to the shamrock on the shirt front. Charlie only ever played the French once, in 1910, so we can be pretty confident that this shirt originates from that match. Who wore it, we can't say. Perhaps one day another researcher will be able to add that detail. Similarly, it is likely that the English shirt in the collection comes from Charlie's very last international appearance in 1910 – the very first international at 'Twickers'. All in all, the shirt collection gives us an insight into a great sporting career, and manages to tell the story of the development of the game itself. It is strange to reflect that when Charlie started playing for Newport in 1901 the game in international terms was only thirty years old.

The convention of shirt-swapping became a rugby tradition before it was established in the sport of football. Shirts were first exchanged after an international football match in 1931, when a France side beat England for the first time. As in rugby, an exchange of shirts has become a ritual after football matches, an expression of sporting camaraderie. The iconic shot of Bobby Moore and Pelé swapping shirts in the 1970 World Cup has become one of sport's most famous images. Both men are wreathed in smiles, clearly at ease in the company of each other's greatest opponent. Despite the 1-0 defeat, the mood in the England camp towards the shirt swap was in marked contrast to the end of the ill-tempered semi-final in 1966. Sir Alf Ramsay, angry at the Argentine 'animals', snatched Geoff Hurst's shirt from the hands of Alberto Gonzalez. To a traditionalist like Ramsay, shirts were earned by his players through

hard work, and were worn with pride. Giving them away to a team that had shown his players such scant respect stuck in his craw. For much of the twentieth century there was little financial motivation to exchange shirts in either sport, although then as now they could be used to raise money at charity dinners. In the money-spinning, corporate-driven twenty-first century, the shirts with the names of Messi or Ronaldo might change hands for huge sums of money.

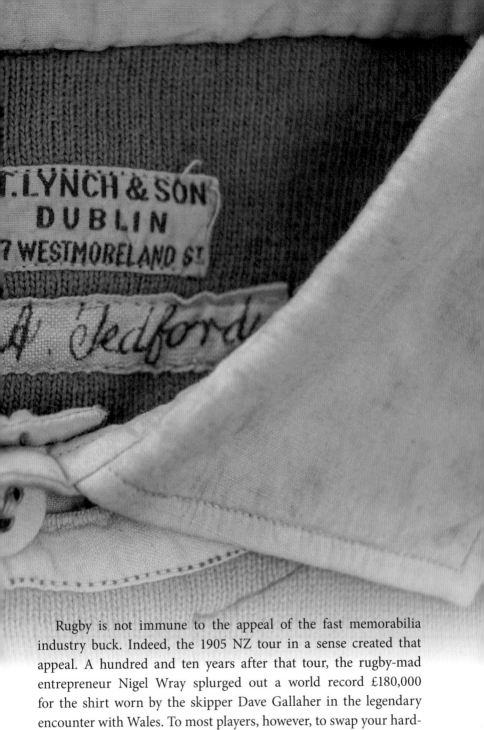

Rugby is not immune to the appeal of the fast memorabilia industry buck. Indeed, the 1905 NZ tour in a sense created that appeal. A hundred and ten years after that tour, the rugby-mad entrepreneur Nigel Wray splurged out a world record £180,000 for the shirt worn by the skipper Dave Gallaher in the legendary encounter with Wales. To most players, however, to swap your hard-won shirt is a mark of mutual respect. The pride you experience in pulling on that shirt represents all the years of training you've put in, the yards of grass you've fought for and the aches and pains you'll suffer for days after the final whistle. Now, at the end of the match, your opponent wants to share that sense of pride. It is another deeply personal way of saying 'well played'. Conor Murray, the Munster, Ireland and Lions scrum-half has said that he only has two framed opposition shirts, those of two of his best opponents – All Black Aaron Smith and Wales' Mike Phillips. Keeping those shirts is a respectful tilt of the hat towards the scrum-halves he considers to have been his toughest adversaries. Murray, in common with all modern players, would have access to a great many shirts. Most international sides now give each player a playing shirt and a spare. This extra shirt could be exchanged with the opposition, or signed in the dressing room to be given away for auction to a favoured charity. Such acts of kindness generate thousands of pounds for deserving causes each year. Inevitably, this can lead to the shirt currency being debased. During the 2017 Lions tour of New Zealand, coach Warren Gatland noted that some provincial opposition players had been involved in some sharp practice. 'Most of their players came in and swapped their official jerseys,' he said 'but four or five of them used replicas.' Those shirts were dampened to make it look as though they had been worn in the match. eBay is a cruel mistress.

In Charlie's case, he saw the potential for his team-mates to turn out in his collection of shirts as a way of entertaining the Rodney Parade faithful. The resulting gate receipts, he knew, could help various causes in his home town. In the 1911 match, the church roof at St John's Maindee was his named charity, and in 1912, a similar match was dedicated to raising funds for the local rowing club. Charlie knew that the wider Newport community would benefit from such an act of selflessness. Some might have seen it as part rugby encounter and part fashion show, a chance to see a famous array of shirts worn by some local legends, although just five minutes in opposition with Newport rugby legends George Boots or Jehoida Hodges would serve to refocus that particular perspective on the game. Accounts of these so-called 'charity matches' show that they were full-blooded affairs. Indeed, some of the shirts do have blood stains, browned over time, as well as the ingrained Rodney Parade mud that the local laundry business run by Welsh skipper Gwyn Nicholls had failed to shift.

Above all, Charlie was a Newport man. There are two Newport 1st XV black and amber shirts in the collection. The older one is threadbare at the shoulders, the fabric battered and worn by hundreds of collisions and scrums. The more recent one is less battered, the colours sharper. The state of this shirt reflects the fact that injury robbed Charlie of game time in his last three seasons. Despite that fact, he would have been immensely proud that the word 'Captain' was inked in alongside his name.

Perhaps it was Charlie's influence as captain on the Football Committee at Rodney Parade that led to an agreement that the club should pay for a set of jerseys, although the minutes do add that the players would still be 'paying for washing and repairs.' This was in 1911, in the final few weeks of Charlie's playing career. His time as a rugby player had seen the Newport and Wales star 'Monkey' Gould embroiled in scandal, England rugby torn apart by the schism with the Northern League, disputes over gate receipts after internationals involving touring sides and many, many of his compatriots drifting to rugby league in order to put food on the table. For his club to finally pay for a player's shirt may seem a small thing over a hundred years later, but Charlie would know that his fellow Black and Amber players would appreciate the gesture. By way of contrast, in the Scottish changing room before the 1920 international against France, the veteran one-eyed Watsonians prop Jock Weymus had asked the management why the other fourteen players had been issued with a new jersey before kick-off. He was asked, quite seriously, about the whereabouts of his 1914 season jersey. Quite apart from reinforcing some completely unfounded Scottish stereotypes, this little exchange shows that for much of the twentieth century the pace of change in the administration of rugby was glacial. The seeds of later disputes over 'Shamateurism' were sown during Charlie's career.

The solid family home on Llwynderi Road is testament to the success of Charlie's work in the wine wholesale business that was based in the town. The 'Newport and South Wales Wine and Spirit Co. Ltd' had been taken over by the Pritchards in 1886 from the Harrhy family. With offices at 10 Cambrian Road, and a store on the High Street, the business prided itself on being the oldest in Newport. In common with all rugby players until the arrival of professionalism in 1995, Charlie had to balance his sporting ambitions with the economic realities of life. His commitment to the business and to his young family meant that he may have missed out on some touring opportunities along the way. Throughout his life Charlie took his responsibilities seriously, at home, on the field of play and in the trenches.

The writer Barbara Tuchman once said that 'The Great War of 1914-18 lies like a band of scorched earth dividing that time from ours.' Over a hundred years after his death, Charlie's shirts have been taken out of the attic of a house in deepest Dorset and are now in the possession of the World Rugby Museum at Twickenham, where he played international rugby for the very last time. Just six-and-a-half years after that match, this gentle, affable man was bleeding to death at a field hospital in war-torn France. The Pritchard Collection not only gives us a unique insight into rugby history, but also connects us to that pre-1914 world through the story of an iconic character who perished in that dreadful conflict.

WALES

'Rugby is part of the DNA of Welshmen and women across the globe. It is at the heart of our very essence, defining us as individuals and as a nation.'

Gareth Edwards

On the extreme left of the photograph taken before the charity match of 1911 is the figure of David ('Dai') Boots. A full-back at Newport RFC between 1899 and 1907, he had seen the young Charlie Pritchard come into the Rodney Parade side and then establish himself as an international player. Blessed as they were with full-backs such as Bert Winfield, the Welsh selectors never brought Dai into the Welsh team. Charlie's charity match, however, gave him the opportunity to play in the hallowed red shirt. Charlie, of course, chose to play the charity game in the All Black shirt he had exchanged on that famous day in Cardiff in December of 1905. Charlie's cap, given to him in recognition of his debut for Wales against Ireland in 1904, is also in the Pritchard Collection, and we have to assume that the shirt that Dai is wearing is from the same game. Charlie wore the red of Wales on 14 occasions between 1904 and 1910, when they were generally acknowledged to be the best of the Home Nations Championship sides, and had some claim to being the best in the world.

As a nation, Wales emerged into the light of the twentieth century in a confident mood. Ports such as Cardiff and Newport were booming and the traditional heavy industries driving the economy forward relentlessly. Workers poured into the Valleys from rural Wales to the north and the west, and there was a steady flow of economic migrants crossing the Severn. The population of the Principality doubled in the last thirty years of the nineteenth century, with the heartland of the Rhondda showing a tenfold increase. These people were absorbed into the tight-knit valley communities, forming fresh supplies of miners and steelworkers, as well as talent for the rugby clubs. The extent of the economy's dependence on coal was not too closely examined for another generation, when the hardships of the 1920s and 1930s brought the bust that followed the boom. It is interesting to note that Welsh rugby's fortunes effectively mirrored the economy, with the success of the pre-war golden age in stark contrast to the years in the wilderness between the wars, when Wales failed to win a championship between 1922 and 1931.

In 1905, the twentieth century was a shiny new coin, and it was in Welsh rugby's pocket. Crowds were up, so the WRU's coffers had doubled by the end of 1905. They had even invested in a new typewriter for the Honorary Secretary. Gloucester's Dai Gent, writing in 1927, said that in his experience Wales were playing 'the most perfect form of rugby I have ever seen.' This from a scrum-half who had plumped for the Red Rose, and who had played the 1905 All Blacks on his international debut for England. Gent admired the instinctive nature of the golden age Welsh side, as well as the club sides that fed it, saying that to an opponent it felt as though the Welsh possessed a 'team telepathy'.

Whatever the truth of the claim that Welsh teams operated on some alternative, ethereal level, there can be no doubting the fact that the sides they put into the field in the first decade of the new century showed tremendous team spirit. Much of the credit for this must go to the captain, Gwyn Nicholls. The heartbeat of the side from 1896 to 1906, he learned his craft at centre the hard way, attempting to shackle Newport's multi-talented Arthur 'Monkey' Gould. Nicholls compared the task of doing so to chasing a butterfly with a hat pin, but he emerged a better defensive player. Nicholls was in the forefront of the development of the role of the centre three-quarter. At Cardiff, and then with Wales, he pioneered the move to

employing two centres. The forwards probably didn't thank him for it in the early years as his seven-man packs fought against grinning opposition eights. Gradually, even forwards became converts to the new system as the power and guile of 'Prince Gwyn' shredded opposition defences. He had played his first game for Cardiff at the tender age of eighteen in February 1893, eventually scoring 111 tries in 242 appearances for the club. The Welsh selectors had come calling in 1896, and he toured Australia with a British team (a precursor of the Lions) in 1899. Towards the end of his career, Nicholls looked for opportunities to set his wingers free, and he placed great emphasis on the timing and accuracy of his passing. He created a potent centre partnership with his Cardiff colleague, 'Rusty' Gabe, whose clever angles of running and explosive pace dovetailed perfectly with his skipper's passing skills. In 1939 Gabe reflected on his playing career, and on the role Nicholls had played in his own success. Nicholls, he said, 'was the complete centre three-quarter.' Gabe also commented on his ability to forge a team, saying that Nicholls had the 'unfailing support of every man on his side.' In the middle of the eighteenth century Samuel Johnson had attempted a definition of genius, and likened it to 'the fire in the flint'. Gwyn Nicholls was undoubtedly the fire in this Welsh side's flint.

The fact that Gabe appeared alongside Nicholls in 1905 was accidental – his tackle on George Davies in a London Welsh versus Swansea encounter meant that the Swansea centre was sidelined for weeks and Gabe was drafted into the Welsh midfield, having initially being capped as a winger. Teams evolve, players come and go. It is often during such moments when all the deliberations of the selectors are rendered pointless that new talent is unearthed and new combinations forged. Gabe and Nicholls became one of the truly great centre combinations to have graced a rugby field. It was entirely fitting that Gabe should be the guest of honour at the opening of the Gwyn Nicholls Memorial Gates at the Cardiff Arms Park on Boxing Day 1949.

Nicholls' emphasis on the team ethos meant that new arrivals felt supported, but also aware of their responsibilities to the other 14 players. 'If any player in any position in a rugby game stands out head and shoulders over his fellows then that player is inevitably THE weak point of the side,' Nicholls once said. He surrounded himself with players of considerable individual brilliance but showed them by his own example that they had a job to do for the team. Such an approach, said Nicholls, would result in a side that off the pitch would be able to discuss tactics together, and would grow to understand each other on the pitch. 'In an ideal Welsh game you really see fifteen great chess masters working in partnership and without consultation,' he once observed. Really good sides leave the opposition wondering if there is a sixteenth man on the pitch. The teams that played the other great golden age Welsh team of the 1970s used to regularly make that observation. Of all the team sports, the ability to read a situation or run a different line can make all the difference in a tight rugby match. Perhaps this was the 'team telepathy' that Dai Gent alluded to, but it was an environment with which the young Charlie Pritchard was familiar at Rodney Parade under TC Graham. As the skipper at Rodney Parade, and a Welsh international on a dozen occasions, Tom Graham played a key role in developing the winning ethos at the club. Pritchard fostered the same approach when he took over the captaincy at Newport.

Once asked to describe the perfect 'system' to adopt when playing the game, Nicholls' response was music to the ears of the rugby purists. 'There isn't one,' he said. 'The one thing necessary is love for the game – to realise that it is the grandest, most glorious and scientific of all games.' Flexibility was key – in December 1905 the Welsh asked a centre, Cliff Pritchard, to play the roving extra forward role in order to neutralise the work of Dave Gallaher. The Pontypool man played his role to perfection, proving to be a keystone of the Welsh defensive effort. He was also the player who picked Dickie Owen's pass off his bootlaces to release Gabe and Morgan to score the crucial try. Cliff was actually Charlie's cousin, and had played for five seasons at Rodney Parade before moving to Pontypool. When Charlie's first son was born in 1904, he was named after him.

Outside the centres Nicholls and Gabe were two whippets – Willie Llewellyn and Teddy Morgan. Although he was at the end of his international career by 1905, Llewellyn had scored 20 international tries and had a good working relationship with his skipper. Already looking ahead to life beyond rugby, he had opened a pharmacy in his home town of Tonypandy by the end of 1905. Five years later, his shop front was the only one left strangely intact when the Riots passed along the main street. His fellow winger, Teddy Morgan, was generally acknowledged to be one of the fastest players on the rugby scene, and, as the All Blacks were to discover, he was a lethal finisher. Behind them, the sure defence and immense boot of Bert Winfield gave the backs the freedom to attack. He may have lacked the attacking flair of a JPR Williams, but on that December day in 1905 Bert's raking touch-finders did much to blunt the All Black game plan.

At half back, there was an embarrassment of riches. The much-admired Newport scrum-half, Tommy Vile, would have to wait until 1908 before he could play in the red of Wales. By that time, he had already played for the British Isles. Dai Gent crossed the Severn to seek international football. This was all because the man in possession of the jersey was Dickie Owen, Swansea's 'Mighty Midget' whose rocket-propelled passes and clever game management made him one of the first names on the team sheet. It was Owen's reverse pass that freed the Welsh midfield in the first half of the All Black game, resulting in Teddy Morgan's try in the corner. Indeed, the whole move had been Owen's contribution to pre-match training. The fact that it worked so spectacularly well underlined why Nicholls had such faith in him. He was the sort of chess-playing half-back that appealed to the skipper. Despite his diminutive stature, Owen dealt with the physical challenge of having roving forward Dave Gallaher on his case in the 1905 fixture. In doing so, he confounded the critics who fully expected the All Black skipper to snuff out the threat posed by the Swansea man. Diminutive he certainly was, but Owen was a steelworker, and his playing record shows that he was fully able to deal with the physical side of the game. Perhaps this was one player the All Blacks underestimated, because his dancing feet always caused the opposition problems around the fringes of the set piece.

Owen played for Wales on 35 occasions between 1901 and 1912, but there was less certainty from the selectors about his half-back partner. The other half of Swansea's 'Dancing Dicks', Dick Jones, was picked on 15 occasions between 1900 and 1910 largely on the basis that he was Owen's usual partner. Selectors were naturally nervous of bringing new half-backs together on the day of a game and expecting them to 'click'. Familiarity bred some content, perhaps, and the fact that the All Whites had gone unbeaten for much of 1904 and 1905 would have also influenced their thinking. The much-vaunted Welsh fly-half factory had been in operation, however, and the selectors tried the two outstanding talents of the age in harness with Owen – Billy Trew and Percy Bush. Trew was also a Swansea player, and his talents secured him 29 caps during the golden age era, Dai Gent describing him as 'easily the finest player I ever saw.' In December 1905, however, the selectors gave the nod to Cardiff's Percy Bush. Exciting and infuriating from one week to the next, Bush had the 'X Factor' the Welsh yearn for in their fly-halves. In modern terms, there is no doubting that the Welsh side of 1905 would have had a strong bench.

As well as popping in to a mythical fly-half factory, the Welsh selectors would, in times of need, be able to whistle down the nearest mine shaft in order to summon a suitable forward. In front of this dazzling back line, the Welsh had been able to choose from a deep pool of talent in the forwards. The hard, physical work in the pits, factories and steelworks meant that the clubs of South Wales were producing big tough men – the so-called 'Rhondda Forwards'. In the early twentieth century the members of the pack would simply appear as 'forward' in the match programmes, as specialist positions were only just being developed. The hard physical nature of the game, allied to the fact that substitutions were not allowed, meant that a turn of the century rugby forward needed to be as tough as teak. Typical of such men was Dai Jones of Treherbert, a forward who was nicknamed 'Tarw', the Welsh word for a bull. At over six feet tall, Jones weighed in at nearly 16 stone. He had followed his father into the coal mines of the Rhondda Valley, and was capped at the age of just twenty in 1902. He went on to play for Wales 13 times, but became one of the players discarded by the selectors after the lacklustre defeat to the touring Springboks in 1906. 'Tarw' became a policeman but was soon on the wrong side of rugby law when he was found to have been taking payments to play at Aberdare RFC. He moved to rugby league, becoming the first player to have beaten the New Zealanders in both codes. Sadly, he was badly wounded on the Somme, and died early and in constant pain in 1933. In his heyday in 1905, however, his combination with 'Boxer' Harding gave the

Welsh scrum the weight, aggression and rugby intelligence it needed to challenge Gallaher's pack.

The core of the Welsh pack was built around what the authors of *Fields of Praise*, the history of Welsh rugby up to 1981, called a 'Newport legacy.' Risca-born Jehoida Hodges played 23 games in the red shirt of Wales between 1899 and 1906. He was noted for his turn of speed, and appeared as a replacement winger against England in 1903. He bagged a hat-trick in the first half, but after the match confessed that 'on the whole I think I would rather play in the pack.' Once a forward, always a forward. The Welsh forwards were unexpectedly successful at the scrummages in the Test against the All Blacks, heeling the ball cleanly so that Owen could release his backs. Dickie Owen, in a lecture a year later, said that it was Swansea's Will Joseph who devised a method of scrummaging which would enable the Welsh pack to channel their ball smartly, presumably in an effort to minimise Gallaher's opportunities to disrupt possession. As well as showing distinct tactical nous, Joseph was a steelworker and a leading light at his local Sunday School. A classically Welsh package, one might say.

The 1905 All Blacks have been rightly lauded over the past hundred years or so as innovators. Their scientific approach to the set piece, in particular, changed the way the game was to be coached and played. In December 1905, however, they came face to face – literally – with one of Welsh rugby's hard nuts. Twyber Travers was a Pill Harriers player who moved up the road to Newport RFC. In the centre of the clubhouse at Pill they had an old coal stove and players would scrummage with their backs to it when it got too dark to practise outside. The shame of retreating at a scrum was quite literally burned into Twyber's soul. In the furious fight to gain the loose-head in the front row, Travers was never going to back down. He did a great deal to define the role of the modern hooker, and his son 'Bunner' carried on the tradition for Wales and the Lions. Newport forward George Boots was also an ever-present figure on the teamsheets in the early years of the century. Having made his debut for Newport in 1895, Boots went on to win 16 Welsh caps

Charlie's Welsh Trial cap, 1903. He gained his full Welsh cap a year later.

between 1898 and 1904. Remarkably, this tough forward played the last of his 365 games for the club at the age of 47. By 1905, Boots had been replaced in the international squad by Rodney Parade's new hero – Charlie Pritchard.

As with the backs, a putative 1905 Welsh bench would be filled with talented forwards. A successful side has to be able to call on good quality replacements. The physical demands of the game may have changed a great deal a century later, but the reality of collisions remains the same. Bone on bone contact will inevitably cause injuries, and a smart coach and his team of selectors need to be constantly scanning the horizon for options. In the great golden age teams there was a consistency of selection, but when change was forced upon them, that change needed to be seamless. Famously, when Gareth Edwards left the field in a match against England in 1970, the Welsh looked doomed. Enter Llanelli's 'Chico' Hopkins, whose try turned the match. Similarly, at the Triple Crown decider at St Helen's against Ireland in 1905, successive injuries to Billy Trew and Dick Jones meant that the selectors had to bring in a youthful half-back from Mountain Ash, Wyndham Jones. He dummied his way to score under the posts in what turned out to be his only Welsh match. Successful sides allow new players to come in and play their game. There was a confidence about Welsh rugby in the 1900s and the 1970s that meant that the teams evolved quite naturally. Like Tommy Vile and many others, Wyndham Jones was destined to play only a small part in that success, with the selectors plumping for the human box of tricks that was Percy Bush to play Gallaher's All Blacks.

The 1905 season came in the middle of a remarkable run of Welsh form, when they were generally acknowledged to be the team to beat in the Home Nations. They won the Championship in 1900, 1902, 1905, 1906, 1908, 1909 and 1911, losing only seven of the 43 matches they played. Before 1905, Wales had won Triple Crowns in 1900 and 1902, but by this time players such as George Boots were at the end of their international shelf life, and Will Osborne's defection to league had created a hole in the 1903 pack. In the Home

Championship of that year, the strong Scottish pack under the leadership of Mark Morrison had carried all before them, taking the Triple Crown for the fourth time. When the Welsh trial teams were gathered together at Tredegar on 5 December 1903, the Welsh selectors had an eye on Charlie Pritchard as the sort of athletic, hard-working forward who might help them to challenge the Scottish pack in the 1904 Championship. Pritchard's trial cap from that day is in the collection.

Another injury to one of the key members of the pack, Dai 'Tarw' Jones, meant that the selectors plumped for the experience of Cardiff's Sam Ramsey in the pack to open the 1904 Home Nations Championship campaign. Strangely enough, it was the Scottish-born forward's second Welsh cap after a disastrous first outing as far back as 1896. The 14-14 draw at Welford Road on 9 January 1904 turned out to be his second and last cap. More pack shuffling followed to meet the Scots at St Helen's on 6 February, where tries by Gabe, Morgan, Brice and Jones resulted in a good 21-3 Welsh win. Charlie waited patiently in the taxi rank line of reserves. The early draw against England meant that a Triple Crown was not achievable, but Wales would have been confident of travelling to the Balmoral Showgrounds in Belfast to play an Irish side that had been comfortably beaten by England and Scotland. On the run up to the match, Charlie travelled with his Newport team-mates to Bristol, and scored a try in a 13-0 win for the Black and Ambers on 27 February. With six days to go until the Ireland match, now named as third reserve, he would have been trying to focus on the game against Swansea on 5 March, feeling that his services would be unlikely to be called upon so late in the day.

As with Charlie's senior debut at Swansea in January 1902, the rugby gods decided to intervene. One by one players dropped out. The 1904 Championship had taken its toll. Two other reserves also dropped out, which meant that Charlie was on the boat to Belfast as a travelling reserve. Then, remarkably, Charlie was elevated to the starting line-up as another player cried off on St David's Day 1904, the day before the game. Just two years after making his senior debut, Rodney Parade's newest star was going to be pulling on the red jersey to face the Irish pack in front of their home crowd.

It was to be the first of Charlie's 14 international caps between 1904 and 1910, which may seem a meagre return to a modern rugby fan. More than a century later, we see international players picking up a dozen caps in a calendar year, allowing for the Six Nations Championship, a summer tour and the autumn internationals. At the start of the twentieth century a Home Nations Championship season would yield three caps (England, Ireland and Scotland), with France on the cusp of entering the competition at the end of Charlie's career. Every year or two, there might be an overseas touring side Test that would result in another cap, so four caps would be the maximum haul for an international player in these years. Furthermore, Charlie was robbed of another ten or so caps after 1908 by a series of injuries as his ferociously committed brand of rugby began to take its toll on his body.

On 2 March 1904 Charlie's dressing room nerves would have been soothed by the presence of his cousin Cliff, the mortician from Pontypool, who had been picked to play in the centre. There were two fellow debutants, but for Howell Jones and Sid Bevan this would be their solitary cap. However Sid did go on tour Down Under with David Bedell-Sivright's British team later in the year and was always able to tell his grandchildren that he had played the legendary All Blacks on their home patch. Howell Jones returned to the Gnoll to lead his excellent Neath side, but the selectors never came calling again. Tragically, Howell died on a rugby pitch just four years later, at the age of just twenty-six, the victim of a stray boot that ruptured his spleen. He never got the chance to see his son Howie win Welsh caps in the 1930s.

The task in hand, however, was formidable. The Irish were cementing their reputation as the Joker in the Home Nations pack, which made them infuriating and exhilarating in turn. On 2 March 1904 a packed Balmoral Showground was treated to a bit of both. Both sides scored four tries as the home team squeaked a 14-12 win. Charlie impressed the rugby aficionados in the press box with a powerful, energetic display of his skills, and he would have enjoyed the challenge of playing against one of Ireland's best forwards, Alfred Tedford. Tedford had scored two tries in the match, and on his return to Ireland in 1906, Charlie secured his shirt after that game. Charlie's debut in 1904 ended with a whiff of controversy about the forward pass call from referee Findlay Crawford that disallowed a Dick Jones match-winning try, and the Welsh had to settle for second place in behind the Scots again. Typically, Charlie played against Swansea just three days later.

Like all his fellow players, and his growing army of fans, Charlie would have to wait until January of 1905 before he could pull on the red shirt of Wales again. In what has gone down in rugby history as one of the great years for Welsh rugby, Charlie and his colleagues secured a fourth Triple Crown as well as defeating the touring All Blacks 3-0 at Cardiff. Wales won the 1905 Championship playing fast, uncompromising rugby, and it is notable that their two wingers, Llewellyn and Morgan, were the top try-scorers of that year. The Welsh campaign yielded 41 points, and their defence only leaked a meagre six. They sounded a warning that this was to be their year by hammering England 25-0, with tries for Morgan, Gabe, Harding, Jones, Llewellyn and Watkins. Frank Stout's Red Rose pack was simply unable to break the stranglehold exerted by Charlie and his fellow forwards.

Next up was a trip to Scotland, where two tries by Willie Llewellyn saw the Welsh home on 4 February.

Charlie's reputation was enhanced in a game which was characterised by the fierce forward exchanges.

The Scots, as the incumbent champions, fought hard but with the Irish having to travel to Cardiff, a Welsh Triple Crown was widely predicted. Just as Charlie was about to play in a Triple Crown decider in only his third senior year of rugby, the injury jinx that was to afflict his later career struck. He sustained an ankle injury in a tight win over the Leicester Tigers at Rodney Parade at the end of February and had to drop out of the Irish match on 11 March. Tries by Wyndham Jones and Teddy Morgan resulted in a 10-3

Copyright Photo by Wills, Cardiff.   Ack Llewelyn, Linesman   Sir J. T. D. Llewelyn, Bart., President, W.R.F.U.
Tom Williams, W.R.F.U.   J. F. Williams   George Travers   Dd. Jones   W. Joseph   R. T. Gabe
C. M. Pritchard   J. J. Hodges   Willie Llewellyn   Gwyn Nicholls, Captain   H. B. Winfield   Cliff Pritchard   A. F. Harding.
Teddy Morgan   R. M. Owen   P. F. Bush.
"Cymru am Byth."   THE WELSH TEAM, which defeated New Zealand Dec. 16th, 1905. by 3 Points to Nil.

win. Charlie managed to get off the treatment table to play Cardiff just a week later, but the narrow 6-3 win against the old enemy will have been tinged with a little frustration at having had to miss the Championship decider. Sadly, it was a feeling that he would have to get used to. A look at Charlie's playing career at Newport gives us a clue. In 1908-09, he managed only six appearances as his knee problems became chronic. Although he made a recovery in his last two seasons, managing over 50 matches in a Newport shirt between 1909 and 1911, the Welsh selectors had been forced to look at other options. There is no doubt that he had been a live contender for captain when Gwyn Nicholls departed the international scene in 1906, but Charlie was simply unable to put in the run of appearances that would make him look like the obvious candidate. The 1905 Championship, however, had established Charlie Pritchard as an international player, and he had taken part in a Triple Crown campaign only three years after his senior debut.

The 1905-06 season would see Charlie at his rampaging best – despite having to step in to take over the Newport captaincy, and his Welsh commitments, Charlie played 27 matches for the Black and Ambers, scoring five tries. He would have been forgiven for holding back a little in the early part of the season in preparation for the challenge of the touring All Blacks, but this was not Charlie's way. He was at the forefront of titanic struggles against Swansea and Cardiff, home and away, in the weeks leading up to the All Blacks game.

In October 1905 the Welsh Match Committee travelled to Gloucester to watch the 'Cherry and Whites' take on Dave Gallaher's men. The 44-0 hammering handed out to the home team must have set alarm bells ringing in the Welsh camp, and furious debates took place behind closed doors. Was this fine, but ageing, Welsh side going to be able to contain the marauding Kiwis? A letter to a local paper from a Cheshire rugby fan reflected on the 34-0 dousing handed out to what was seen as a decent County side.

'Welsh players should invoke in unison the spirit of Druids who haunt the famous Anglesey village of Llanfairpwllgwyngyllgogerychwyrndrobwllllantysiliogogogoch.'

Inside the Welsh camp, the arguments focused on tactics. They had decided to fight fire with fire at scrum time, and began practising a 2-3-2 formation to counter that of the visitors. Cliff Pritchard was earmarked to play the roving extra back\loose forward role in an attempt to counteract Dave Gallaher's overwhelming influence in the loose and in the tight. Although there was a temptation for the Welsh to focus on their own strengths out wide, there was a pragmatic realisation that as with all big rugby matches, there would be a need to attain superiority, or at least parity, in the arm wrestle up front. A big question remained – would the seven-man Welsh pack win enough ball to put skipper Gwyn Nicholls and his back line on the front foot?

A Probables vs Possibles trial match was arranged for 20 November to help the Welsh selectors to make their final decisions, but it was disrupted by several withdrawals. Gloomily the Welsh rugby press reported on the frankly unhelpful 18-9 victory by the Possibles. A second trial match took place on the day that the English were being put to the sword by the All Blacks at Crystal Palace. Ironically, the England scrum-half who was making his debut was the Welsh-qualified Dai Gent, who had in fact played for the Welsh Probables on 20 November. An improved Probables showing this time round resulted in a nerve steadying 33-11 victory. Perhaps Dai Gent had jumped ship a little too early?

On 7 and 12 December training sessions focused on the Welsh scrummage, and Dickie Owen took the backs through a pre-planned move off one of his famous reverse passes. Little did they know just how important those few minutes would prove to be. The very thought of the Swansea man's slight nine-stone frame up against the burly Dave Gallaher was probably giving the Match Committee some nightmares, but this was as well prepared a side as Wales had ever put into the field. The majority of rugby writers would have agreed with 'Captain Fitzgerald' of *The Sporting Life*, who made the marauding Kiwis the favourites for the Cardiff encounter. 'New Zealand will win their match with Wales by their international average, about 14 points, if the Welsh forwards can hold the tourists' scrum. If the latter are, however, masters in the scrum then our Colonial friends will win by a good bit more.' 'Captain Fitzgerald' had pinpointed what the Welsh already knew – that the battle would be won and lost in the forward exchanges. The Welsh pack had steeled themselves to fight for the 'loose-head' in the front row of the scrum, so that their hooker Twyber Travers would be able to strike for the ball cleanly. Scrummaging technique had done much to establish All Black superiority in the tour up to that point. Charlie and his fellow forwards would have to face up to this challenge.

On the day of the match, Charlie and his team-mates would have realised they were playing in a game unlike any other. The febrile atmosphere of Cardiff on that misty afternoon would have been felt down in the dressing room. Like Dickie Owen, Charlie had opted for new white laces in his boots. With the smell of embrocation heavy in the air, and studs clattering on the floor, the players were called in to a tight knot around their inspirational skipper, Gwyn Nicholls. He began to speak.

He ended the team talk thus: 'We have already discussed tactics. So it only remains to me to appeal to you to be resolute in your tackling. You all know what New Zealand are like if they are given latitude. They throw the ball about, and their system of intensive backing up makes them very dangerous. So there must be no hair-combing. Every man in possession must be put down, ball and all. As for the forwards, you already know what to do to get the loose-head. Come on. Let's get out.'

The Welsh team took the field to the roar of the crowd, then stood respectfully, curiously to watch the Haka. The afternoon mist swirled around the combatants. Then Teddy Morgan led the players in their pre-planned response – the singing of 'Hen Wlad fy Nhadau'. It was the first time a national anthem was sung as a curtain-raiser to an international match. Now, of course, it is part of the set protocol, a moment that unites fans and players. In 1905, however, the players had no idea how the crowd would react. The emotion must have been catching in the throats of Charlie and his team-mates as 40,000 voices were lifted to the skies above Cardiff.

"Y Ddraig Goch a ddyry Gychwyn."

COPYRIGHT.

THE OFFICIAL PROGRAMME.

New Zealand
v.
Wales

CARDIFF ARMS PARK,
DECEMBER 16th, 1905.

Printed and Published by Rees' Electric Press, Plymouth Street, Cardiff, in conjunction with the Welsh Football Union.

For these two small nations, this mattered. The 'Eisteddfod of meat, blood and sinew' was about to begin.

From the first whistle by referee John Dallas, it was clear that Gwyn Nicholls' team talk had inspired Charlie. He was always a noted tackler, building a reputation at Rodney Parade for hitting opponents hard and low. On that day, however, he seems to have moved up a notch. Rugby journalist WJT Collins (who used the pen name of 'Dromio' when writing in the *South Wales Argus*), had watched him play a good deal in the previous three years, and picked out Charlie's performance as noteworthy. He said that Pritchard 'performed prodigies of aggressive defence'. In the days when newsprint was the only mass media available to a rugby fan, the analysis of writers such as 'Dromio' would carry tremendous weight. Team mate Twyber Travers also picked Charlie's defence out as a key reason for the Welsh pack's success on the day. 'He knocked 'em down like nine pins,' said the Pill Harriers hard man.

Likewise Charlie's cousin Cliff Pritchard, playing in an unaccustomed role as a 'roving' forward, produced an outstanding defensive display. The *Western Mail* said the Pontypool man's 'deadly tackling was chiefly the means of preventing the attack of the Colonial backs being fully developed ...' Then as now, any side playing the All Blacks has to produce a big defensive performance. Gwyn Nicholls felt that if that could be achieved, his backs had the necessary speed and skill to challenge the tourists. He was proved right. The captain's defence that day was nigh faultless, and his backline's execution of the Teddy Morgan try was a perfect illustration of what England's Jack Raphael meant when he said that the Welsh backs were 'to football what Greek culture is to literature'. The deceptive reverse pass from Dickie Owen, Cliff Pritchard's take and give, Rusty Gabe playing his role as a Mathematics teacher with his fine appreciation of angles – all topped off by Teddy's searing pace. The scoreline of 3-0 to the Welsh hardly does justice to the significance of the achievement. Moreover, Charlie would have seen a leader who led by example. It was an example that he would take to heart, trying to emulate 'Prince Gwyn' on the pitch at Rodney Parade and in the trenches a decade later.

The Welsh players would have been forgiven for feeling that there was a touch of 'After the Lord Mayor's Ball' about the Championship in the spring of 1906. With the All Blacks gone, British rugby was digesting the lessons learned, and looking ahead to the arrival of the South Africans. On 13 January 1906, normal service was resumed as tries by Hodges, Morgan, Maddock and Charlie Pritchard sank the English at Richmond. Charlie celebrated what turned out to be his sole international try by singing a duet with 'Rusty' Gabe on the train home. On 3 February the Welsh won their annual slugfest against the Scots 9-3 to set up another Triple Crown decider against the Irish. The date on the Irish shirt in the Pritchard Collection shows that Charlie swapped his shirt after this game. He chose to approach the hero from the 1904 game, Alfred Tedford, one of the opposing forwards who had scored two tries on Charlie's debut. The 1906 match, however, was a disappointment for the Welsh, as they were beaten at the Balmoral Showgrounds. Tries by Gabe and Morgan were not enough, as the Irish ran out 11-6 winners. Tries by Thrift, Wallace and the white-gloved Basil Maclear sent the Belfast crowd home happy. As points difference was not counted, Wales would have to share the Championship with the celebrating Irish. Honours even, but it was a rueful Welsh side that took the boat home. The fact that Charlie had Tedford's shirt stuffed into his suitcase would have been scant consolation.

The defeat to Paul Roos' Springboks on 1 December 1906 would have given the Welsh selectors more food for thought. Just a year after winning what had been touted as the 'World Championship' match against the All Blacks, the Welsh were now forced to shake things up. Gwyn Nicholls, having returned from a brief self-imposed international exile at the end of the 1906 Home Championship season to 'have a shot at the Springboks', had played his last game for Wales. Although he produced a match-winning performance against the Springboks in the blue and black of Cardiff a month later, he would have regretted not sticking to his decision to call time on his international career after the defeat by the Irish in March 1906. Dai 'Tarw' Jones, Will Joseph and Jack Williams joined 'Prince Gwyn' on the pile of discarded Welsh players. Charlie survived the cull – indeed, he was now seen as one of the team's veterans, a steadying influence in a time of change. It is perhaps significant that it was he who delivered the speech at the post-match dinner.

One of the new faces brought in for the 1907 season was Newport's Billy Dowell, the twenty-two-year-old who had already been blooded against the All Blacks and the Springboks at Rodney Parade. He proved to be a short-term answer, however, as he 'went north' to play league for Warrington after an initial move to Pontypool. For the rest of the century, Welsh rugby would have to face the fact that young players from working class backgrounds would inevitably find the prospect of securing a wage from playing the game they loved an attractive prospect. Billy joined the growing ranks of dual code rugby internationals, and played against the touring rugby league Kangaroos in Warrington's 10-3 victory at Wilderspool in November 1908. Charlie and his team-mates in Newport and in the Welsh set-up would have accepted the reality of the situation. As a businessman, he was able to secure his family's future through the success of the firm. Rugby league would have held no appeal for someone like Charlie, who was soaked in the traditions of his home club.

The 1907 Welsh squad, perhaps still reeling from the defeat by the Springboks, were to suffer more disappointment. This was to be Scotland's year, with tries from Purves and Monteith setting up a crucial 6-3 win against the Welsh in the second round of matches. Wales had already brushed aside the English at St Helen's, Swansea on 12 January with a brace each for Maddock and Williams, as well as scores by Gibbs and Brown. Just over a year after that big day in Cardiff, only three other members of that winning side were sitting in the dressing room with Charlie – Travers, Gabe and the new captain, Dickie Owen.

Cardiff's Johnny Williams scored a hat-trick against the Irish to cement his reputation as one of the best wingers in the land, and

Wales gained some revenge for past defeats by trouncing the Irish 29-0 at Cardiff. Again, however, the last game of the Championship season would have had the taste of flat Guinness, and Charlie and his team-mates would have been frustrated to finish second again.

In 1908 Wales bounced back. They won the Championship by securing another Triple Crown and the arrival of the French meant that they gained the very first 'Grand Slam'. Again, it was a victory against the hapless English that kicked off the international season. This time, 25,000 fans struggled to see much of the Welsh side's 28-18 victory at a foggy Ashton Gate ground in Bristol. Charlie would have been pleased to see his Newport colleague Tommy Vile win a long overdue first cap. At a key moment in the game, there was a scramble for the ball which was won by 'Rusty' Gabe. As he set off for the English line, Percy Bush set off across the pitch in the opposite direction, drawing the English defence with a stream of yells and whoops. By the time the referee made his way through the fog and caught up with Gabe, he was waiting patiently in the English dead ball area, the try scored. Gabe scored once more, and further tries by Bush, Trew and Gibbs left England befuddled.

A week later, on 25 January 1908, Charlie travelled to the County Ground in Exeter to play in a tough 5-0 win for the Black and Ambers. He did not reappear on a rugby pitch until October of that year. His knee problems had been causing him some ongoing concern, but now he was faced with a considerable spell on the sidelines. He would have taken some cheer from Wales' Championship season, but again it would have been a bittersweet feeling. He managed a run of five games through October and November 1908 before the knee broke down again in a rugged encounter with the Gloucester Cherry and Whites at Kingsholm. Again, he was off the field until he turned out against Neath in February 1909, and another international season had passed him by. By now, Newport had turned to Tommy Vile to captain the side, and Charlie must have wondered if he would ever pull on the red shirt of Wales again. Two international Grand Slam seasons had gone by in a nightmare thirteen month period.

Now approaching thirty, he would have been acutely aware that his time may have passed.

The Welsh selectors did not lose faith with the Newport player, however, and he would have been delighted to be picked at the start of the 1910 Championship season. It was a new challenge for Charlie – his first (and last) opportunity to take on a French pack. On New Years' Day 1910 Charlie would have been able to put his injury trouble behind him, and he enjoyed the sight of Cardiff's Reggie Gibbs showing the French defence a clean pair of heels as he helped himself to a hat-trick. Wales won comfortably, 49-14, and Charlie had another shirt for his collection. He had started to organise a charity game at Rodney Parade, where his friends were invited to play in his collection of shirts for various good local causes. As he approached the end of his career, the process of shirt collection would have gathered pace, perhaps, and the pale blue French shirt, with distinctive Olympic rings on its badge, would have made a welcome addition.

Two weeks later, Charlie played at Twickenham, his last international cap. Whether he knew that at the outset, we don't know. He certainly chose a moment of some historical significance to make his curtain call. It was the very first international match at the 'Cabbage Patch'. Tries by Fred Chapman and Barney Solomon were enough to convince the long-suffering English fans that this was a side on an upward curve. The move to Twickenham was, in effect, a statement of intent, and now the English players had shown some belief. Adrian Stoop's side were on the cusp of establishing themselves as the team to beat in the next few seasons. Wales would not beat England at Twickenham until 1933.

Perhaps Charlie saw the writing on the wall. It may well be that the unmistakable message that his knee sent was that it was over. Perhaps he spoke to some of his closest team-mates afterwards and admitted to the pain. Having played with him for so long, and seen him perform at close quarters, perhaps they saw it too. Whatever the truth of the situation, Charlie's mind was made up. He declared himself unavailable for the next match against the Irish, in effect

standing aside so that his Newport team-mate Ernie Jenkins could win his first cap. It was a typical gesture from Pritchard.

There was one last shirt in the collection, which again tells its own story of Charlie's selflessness. In January 1911 he turned out in a Welsh trial match, where the leading candidates for the 1911 Welsh squad would be assessed by the selectors in a competitive game. He did this despite the fact that he had declared himself unavailable, so the selectors knew that he was not an option for the forthcoming England game. The Pritchard Collection features Charlie's shirt from that game at Cardiff. Charlie was one of seven Newport players in the Stripes (or Possibles) team. This core of club team-mates was enough to tip the scales in favour of the Stripes on the day. After a scrappy opening quarter, Charlie's side settled down to play some good rugby. Highlights included some clever interpassing between Walter Martin and Fred Birt that resulted in a try for Llanelli's Evan Davies and a well crafted try for fly-half Martin. The match, as usual, caused the press to grumble over the

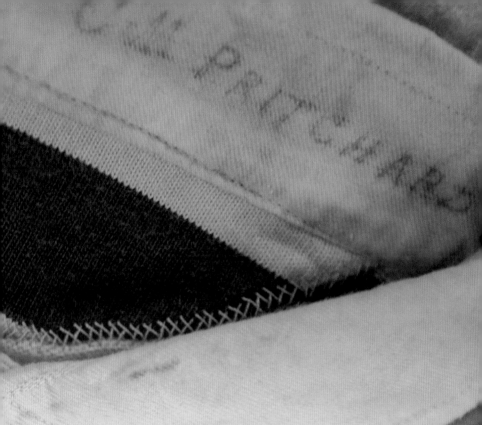

eventual selections, because the Newport half-back pairing of Vile and Martin clearly outperformed the opposition on the day. There were dark mutterings of West Wales bias as several members of the Swansea side failed to even turn up. The *Monmouthshire Football Post* angrily denounced the 'Farce of Welsh Trial Matches'. It was, however, typical of Charlie's ongoing commitment to the cause that he should play. It was also, perhaps, an indication of the fact that the selectors respected his opinion on the emerging talent.

It is interesting to note that the Whites (or Probables) pack that day was led by the Reverend Alban Davies, the hard man of the cloth who would go on to captain the Welsh team immediately before the outbreak of war. The Reverend led Wales' widely-feared pack, known as the 'Terrible Eight'. Famously – or infamously – they took part in a match against the Irish in Belfast that was described as 'the roughest game ever'. Knowing Charlie's views on what constituted fair play it may be that once more Charlie had a view of where the future lay and was happy with the decision he had made.

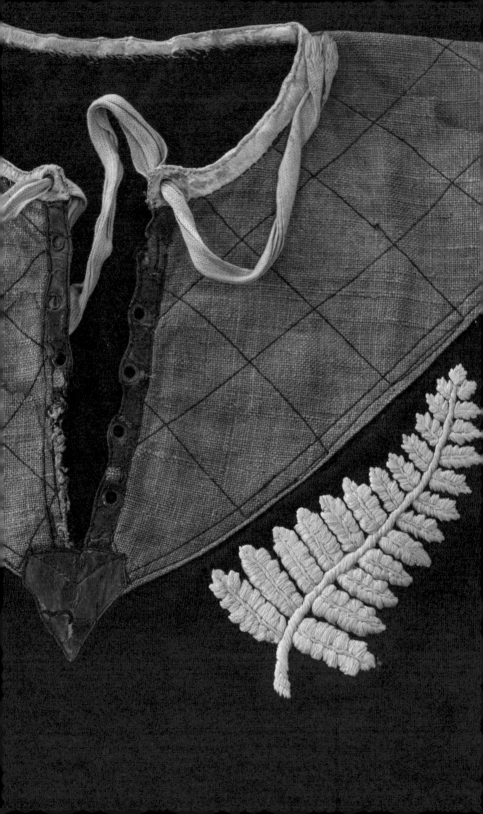

NEW ZEALAND

'The notion that these men beat us because of our physical degeneracy is nonsense. They beat us by organisation and by tactics.'   *CB Fry*

It is no surprise that Charlie should choose to wear the All Black shirt from his collection for the charity match. His sense of pride in being able to lay claim to that famous scalp is palpable. The match was played more than five years after the New Zealanders had set sail for home, but the impact of Dave Gallaher's side on British rugby was still being felt.

The mere restatement of the key facts of the tour – Points For – 976, Points Against – 59 Tries scored – 243 is enough for us to grasp the enormity of their achievement, but Charlie's chest is puffed out in that picture because he knew the truth that lay behind the numbers.

This mere statement of these statistics from the 1905-06 Originals Tour is indeed impressive enough, but when SS Rimutaka left New Zealand on 8 August 1905 no one would have imagined the lasting impression that this group of men would leave on the sport. This collection of foundry workers, farmers, miners and bootmakers was to change the way the game was played.

One of the key topics of conversations revolved around the role played by their redoubtable captain, Dave Gallaher. As a loose forward, he would feed the ball into the New Zealand scrum, then join the set piece in front of the ball. This in effect blocked the

NEW ZEALAND FOOTBALL TEAM,
1905-6.

opposing scrum-half, allowing Gallaher's own half-backs extra time in attack. Their two-man front row formation meant that their hooker always had a free view of the ball, and they established a powerful hold on possession from the set piece. When the opposition was feeding the ball into the scrum, Gallaher would be able to disrupt any moves, as he was not bound onto the scrum. Opposition half-backs must have seen those craggy moustachioed features in their worst nightmares for years afterwards. As a result of these tactics Gallaher became the target for some concerted vilification from crowds and rugby pundits, who felt that bemused referees should be whistling for offside.

The similarities between that situation and the constant grumbling at the way the recently retired All Black skipper Ritchie McCaw operated at the breakdown during his career is quite striking. As a long-time fan of McCaw, it was quite a thrill to hold the No.7 shirt from the Originals tour, and think about the comparisons between the two great loose forwards. But McCaw wore the hallowed No. 7 shirt as a modern open-side flanker, and when Charlie swapped shirts in 1905, the numbering system adopted by the Welsh would have been more familiar to rugby league fans. The player wearing the 1 shirt was the full-back, and one of the forwards would have worn 15. Charlie Pritchard, playing in the pack, wore 12. The numbering system of the All Blacks was different too, with skipper Gallaher wearing number 1 in a squad numbering system. The very idea of putting numbers on their backs was another New Zealand innovation, introduced to help the crowds identify the players, rather than define their positions. The Northern Hemisphere dragged its feet on this issue too. As late as 1928 at Murrayfield James Aitkan Smith was asked by none other than King George V why the players were not identifiable by numbered shirts and the starchy President of the Scottish Rugby Union responded by saying, 'This, Sir, is a rugby match not a cattle sale'. The No. 7 All Black shirt at this 'cattle sale' of 1905 worn so proudly by Charlie in the 1911 charity match at Rodney Parade belonged to the Dunedin-born bank manager Frank Glasgow.

NUMBERS, NAMES AND POSITIONS OF PLAYERS.

NEW ZEALAND v. WALES.

Kick off 2.30 p.m.

WALES.

BACK.—
1 H. B. WINFIELD (Cardiff).

THREE-QUARTER BACKS.—
2 E. G. NICHOLLS (Captain, Cardiff).
3 WILLIE LLEWELLYN (Penygraig).
4 R. T. GABE (Cardiff).
5 E. T. MORGAN (London Welsh).

HALF BACKS.—
6 R. M. OWEN (Swansea).
7 PERCY BUSH (Cardiff).

EXTRA BACK.—
8 CLIFF PRITCHARD (Pontypool).

FORWARDS.—
9 W. JOSEPH (Swansea).
10 G. TRAVERS (Pill Harriers).
11 J. J. HODGES (Newport).
12 C. M. PRITCHARD (Newport).
13 A. F. HARDING (London Welsh).
14 J. F. WILLIAMS (London Welsh).
15 D. JONES (Aberdare).

NEW ZEALAND.

BACK.—
15 G. GILLETT (Canterbury).

THREE-QUARTER BACKS.—
14 W. J. WALLACE (Wellington).
13 R. G. DEANS (Canterbury).
12 D. McGREGOR (Wellington).

FIVE-EIGHTHS.—
11 H. J. MYNOTT (Taranaki).
10 J. HUNTER (Taranaki).

HALF BACK.—
9 J. ROBERTS (Wellington).

FORWARDS.—
8 S. CASEY (Otago).
7 F. GLASGOW (Taranaki).
6 F. NEWTON (Canterbury).
5 J. O'SULLIVAN (Taranaki).
4 G. TYLER (Auckland).
3 A. M'DONALD (Otago).
2 C. SEELING (Auckland).
1 D. GALLAHER (Wing, Capt., Auckland).

Referee—MR DAVIES (Scotland).

Linesman—G. H. DIXON (President New Zealand), ACK LLEWELLYN (Pontypridd).

The scrum was another area where the Originals were going to challenge the established order. Prior to their arrival on our shores, the formation of the scrummage was a matter of 'First Up, First In' – in other words, scrummaging formation was not set in specialist positions. As a forward like Charlie, you might be in the front row for one scrum, then you would arrive at the next breakdown to find the front row already locking horns, and you would bind up in the second row. As the New Zealanders practised their scrummaging, so they were the first to understand the need to form up in the most effective unit. Similarly, they practised lineouts, targeting the best jumpers in the pack rather than simply restarting the game with a hopeful lob into a crowd of players. Out in the backs, their development of the 'five-eighths', linking forwards to backs, gave them more freedom in attack. As today, the All Black approach to rugby was scientific and innovative.

So it was that despite their weeks at sea, the tourists exploded on the sporting scene in the autumn of 1905 by trouncing some reputedly strong sides. Their outstanding back, Billy 'Carbine' Wallace scored three tries as they raced to a 55-point lead at Exeter against Devon. He was so relaxed that he played much of the game in a hat to keep the sun out of his eyes. When the news reached London, so the story goes, a stunned sub-editor assumed the score had been reversed – surely the powerful ex-County Champions Devon had won 55-4? This was just one of the tales that became part of the mythology created by this All Black tour.

Nine matches followed in the next month, and the scores mounted as the scalps of some England's finest rugbying sides were taken. Cornwall 0 New Zealand 41; Bristol 0 New Zealand 41; Northampton 0 New Zealand 32; Leicester 0 New Zealand 28; Middlesex 0 New Zealand 34; Durham 3 New Zealand 16; Hartlepool 0 New Zealand 63; Northumberland 0 New Zealand 31; Gloucester 0 New Zealand 44. The *Daily Mail* gnashed its teeth at the thought of mere Colonials dealing out such humiliating defeats, and blamed it all on a moral and physical decline at the heart of the nation. 'Has the decadence of the English athlete really set in?' it cried. In

A DASH FROM A

The Rugby football team from New Zealand has signalised its appearance in this country by defeating the county teams by unprecedented scores. On Wednesday of last w
combination of the New Zealanders proved too much for the home team. Th

NDERS V. MIDDLESEX AT STAMFORD BRIDGE.

THE MIDDLESEX GOAL

DRAWN BY ERNEST PRATER

...ir first appearance in London at Stamford Bridge Grounds, defeating Middlesex County team by 34 points to none. The match was well fought out to a finish, but the scientific ...rm is entirely black with a leaf badge. The Middlesex wore their striped jerseys more measured, knowledgeable terms, sporting icon and writer CB Fry put it down to superior organisation and tactics. Britain's High Commissioner to New Zealand, W Pember Reeves told *The Times* that 'There is nothing mystical about this team's success. It is to do with speed and agility. They move the ball as if everyone was a three-quarter. They play with both ends – their heads and feet.' Again, it is striking to the modern rugby fan how easily these words could be quoted in a commentary box after a match between a home nation and the All Blacks over a hundred years later.

None of this would have cowed Charlie Pritchard. He had been brought up at Rodney Parade under the influence of the great Tom Graham, who initiated what the rugby pundit 'Dromio' described as a 'school for footballers' in the 1890s, and won 12 caps for Wales. His belief in the development of an all-round game sounds enlightened, even a century later. 'Why cannot a forward handle and pass the ball as accurately as a half-back or a three-quarter?' he asked. A Geordie by birth, Graham encouraged players like Charlie to think and discuss tactics during their sessions. He also asked them to forego alcohol when in training. To a modern eye, this all looks very 'professional', until you see that there was a club allowance for cigarettes so that players could smoke to their hearts' content when they were on the train to away matches.

The river of All Black points flowed on into the winter of 1905. Eventually it swept away international teams too. The Scots, who looked down their patrician noses at these tourists who were being paid an allowance, were defeated 12-7 at Inverleith. The Originals experienced what it was like to be behind on the scoreboard for the first time on tour, but finally conquered the feisty Scottish forwards and the ice rink conditions to score four tries. One of the tries was scored by Frank Glasgow, the wearer of the No. 7 shirt from Charlie's collection, and there was a brace for the elusive winger George Smith. A week later they were in Dublin, where Donegal's own son, Dave Gallaher, was given a hero's welcome. The hospitality of the Irish was in marked contrast to the response of the Scots, who had not even invited the tourists to their after-match dinner. In front of 12,000 at Lansdowne Road, the All Blacks had to work hard once more to contain the opposition forwards, but eventually ran out comfortable winners by 15 points to nil.

Another lengthy journey by sea and land brought the exhausted tourists back to London. They emerged from the dressing room on 2 December 1905 to be faced by a record-breaking crowd. The official capacity of the stadium was 50,000, but at least another 20,000 had crammed into Crystal Palace to see the match. England had chosen to blood eight new caps, and their inexperience was cruelly exposed on a day that saw New Zealand's Duncan McGregor score four tries in another comfortable 15-0 win. Gallaher was plainly puzzled by the England selection. 'From our experience, we did not think that this side was fully representative of the best men to be found in the country,' he said later. Although he was only half-fit after the injury that kept him on the sidelines at Lansdowne Road, Gallaher's domination around the fringes made life all but impossible for John Raphael to launch any meaningful English attacks. It is sad to note that both these great sportsmen were killed in 1917, near Ypres, and now lie in cemeteries just a couple of miles apart on the outskirts of Poperinge.

The fact that Gallaher was carrying an injury was a clear sign that the touring party was beginning to suffer the consequences of their punishing schedule. They had played 27 matches in just 88 days. Now, after three internationals on successive weekends, with midweek matches thrown in, the New Zealanders arrived in Wales. The rugby writers sharpened their pencils. Now, they thought, we'll see what these Colonials are made of.

Inevitably, the exhausted tourists had dropped to sleep by the time the train came into Cardiff station just before midnight on 14 December 1905. A respectful team of officials were waiting on the platform, ready to relay the men to the waiting carriages that would take them to the Queen's Hotel on the Westgate. As they approached the hotel, the nodding New Zealanders were startled by a huge crowd of enthusiastic rugby supporters. Now they knew they were in Wales. In just two days they would be playing another international, but they knew instinctively that this would not be as straightforward as the games at Dublin and Crystal Palace. There was a fervour about these fans who had turned up in the middle of the night that reminded them of home.

Cardiff on match day is on every modern rugby fan's bucket list. The swirl of fans in the streets around the stadium would of course have looked different in 1905 – flat caps and ties would be replaced over a century later by inflatable daffodils and replica shirts – but the pulse of the crowd would be the same. There would have been a palpable sense of excitement on the morning of 16 December 1905 as the trains bearing the fans flowed down the valleys and the city centre started to fill up. Then, as now, individuals hunted down friends and family, then marched off to one of the city's watering holes to share their thoughts over a beer. Would Gallaher rule the roost in midfield? Could the Welsh scrum hold out, and give 'Prince Gwyn' Nicholls enough ball to weave a bit of magic? Was it a big game too far for a number of ageing Welsh stars? Fundamentally, as rugby fans, they were excited by the prospect of seeing this Kiwi side in the flesh. Both sides sensed something about the other – rugby was one of the ways in which these small countries would make their mark on the world. New Zealanders and Welshmen define their sense of otherness through the game, and the contest of 1905 was a meeting of two peoples whose hearts beat to the same rhythm.

The gates at the Arms Park opened at 11am, and they closed on a capacity crowd at 1.30pm. Boys scrambled up trees to gain vantage points, and at the base of each tree a knot of ticketless fans would be getting breathless updates throughout the match. At 2.20pm the formidable figure of Dave Gallaher led his side out onto the pitch, then there was a deafening roar as Gwyn Nicholls led out the men in red. The Welsh captain, straight-backed as ever, would have given no hint of nerves as he marched out. Despite a correspondent in *The Times* noting that he favoured the visiting team because 'the rugby game is always the prerogative of youth', the veteran centre must have been energised by the crowd. For all the old heads in his side, he knew that he could also depend on the more youthful commitment of men like Charlie Pritchard. His side was as well prepared as it could be, and perhaps Nicholls was quietly confident that this was to be his day.

After the Haka had been performed, Welsh hearts would have swelled to bursting point when the crowd joined in a rendition of 'Hen Wlad fy Nhadau'. The modern fan would enjoy the full throated delivery of the rival anthems as part and parcel of the build up to an international match. The Welsh singing on that day in December 1905 was the start of that tradition. Its effect even today, under the roof of the ultra-modern Principality Stadium, is likely to move grown men to tears, so the power of the singing of the hymn that day can only be imagined. The correspondent with New Zealand's *Lyttelton Times* described it as 'the most impressive incident I have ever witnessed on a football field. It gave a semi-religious solemnity to this memorable contest ... It was a wonderful revelation of the serious spirit in which the Welsh take their football.' The All Blacks were taking on a nation.

Another of Rodney Parade's favoured sons, Jehoida Hodges, kicked off, and the crowd watched as the titanic struggle unfolded. The boys up in the trees would have tried to convey the passion and ferocity of the opening exchanges, but soon that task became easier as the game settled into a rhythm. The All Black tactic of kicking into the Welsh backfield was nullified by the raking return kicks of Cardiff's Bert Winfield at full-back, and the Welsh began to exert some control. At scrum time, the Welsh had pulled a rabbit from the hat in tactical terms. The All Black front row was faced not with three men, but two. As a ferocious battle to hook the ball by establishing the loose-head evolved, the Welsh countered Gallaher's men by sending a third man – the 'loose-head'- in to the fray. It was a tactic that surprised the All Blacks, who struggled to answer this challenge legally, and they gave away a stream of penalties. Eventually, Gallaher gave an order that they should just allow the Welsh to have the ball, and depend on their counterattacking to win the game. It was a brave but ultimately the wrong call.

Starved of ball, and constantly pinned back in their half by Winfield's touch finders, the All Blacks were beginning to sense that the writing was on the wall. A Welsh scrum formed up fifteen yards in from the right and some forty yards out from the Kiwi try line. Dickie Owen decided it was time to play his own trump card. Nicholls passed the call on to his back line. Percy Bush at fly-half looked to be setting up an attack down the narrower blind side of the pitch. Nicholls drifted across to the blind in order to draw more of the All Black defence. Owen feinted to his right, seemingly intent on attacking down that channel, then swivelled, throwing out a long reverse pass to his left. Charlie's cousin Cliff, whose contributions to the game up till this point had been purely defensive, picked the ball up off his toes, swerved round a would-be tackler, then set off into lightly defended Kiwi territory. As scrum-half Fred Roberts and his back row struggled to plug the gap caused by Owen's wrong-footing manoeuvre, Pritchard passed to centre 'Rusty' Gabe. He straightened his line to hold the defenders out wide then passed on to Teddy Morgan. By this time, Arthur 'Monkey' Gould, the game's first superstar and now a selector, was clambering onto a press table and waving his hat. 'The fastest Rugby sprinter in the world! Teddy Morgan has scored!' It was the winning score, the only score on the day. Beautifully constructed, it showed that old heads can win rugby matches by making the right decisions at the right time.

The All Black response was typical of Gallaher's men. They upped the tempo and produced a subtle change of tactics. The kicks were shorter and lower in an effort to make Winfield rethink his positioning, and to give the forwards more of an opportunity to pressurise the Welsh defence. Despite this, the Kiwi backs were drained of confidence, and their attacks petered out. At half-time, the crowd were in good voice. Charlie and his colleagues knew they had the measure of the visitors, and soaked up the singing from the terraces. Gallaher and the men in his huddle had all the problems, and a vanishing sense of self belief that they could fix them. The score was only 3-0, but the Welsh had created all the chances.

So it continued into the second half. The Welsh pack, with

Charlie outstanding, were described by one journalist as 'like terriers after a rat'. The intensity of the Welsh effort was waxing rather than waning, although any team that feels as though it is justifiably on top in such a tight contest is always aware that one score, one moment of brilliance, could deprive them of their great day. Pritchard's tackling was considered by many judges to be one of the deciding factors. WJT Collins ('Dromio') wrote that Charlie's "prodigies of aggressive defence" was the key to the eventual Welsh success. It was this relentless ferocity that kept the All Blacks at bay.

Eventually, however, there was the moment of brilliance that everyone had been waiting for. A Welsh kick over the top was scooped up by 'Carbine' Wallace on the wing. Nicknamed after a famous race horse, Wallace was a rugby thoroughbred, and he set off on an arcing counterattack. He punctured the hitherto solid Welsh line by straightening his angle of running to take him between centres Nicholls and Gabe. Full-back Bert Winfield was now in his sights, and an increasingly desperate Welsh defence was scrambling behind him. Wallace slowed up a fraction to weigh up his options, then threw a pass to Bob Deans. What happened in the following few seconds has gone down in rugby mythology.

Deans was still thirty yards out, and Teddy Morgan, the fastest man on the park, was closing the gap. The New Zealander inadvertently made Morgan's task easier by angling his run in towards the posts, probably thinking that if he got close to the Welsh posts a conversion would win the game. Fatefully, it was enough to allow Morgan to bisect his path, and Deans was hauled to the turf. A few seconds later, referee Dallas awarded a scrum, convinced that Deans had grounded the ball short of the Welsh try line. Deans was incensed, convinced he had scored, but then had been dragged back. A deeply religious man, Deans had made it his business to knock on the cabin doors of his team-mates on the long sea voyage from New Zealand so that he could muster a decent showing at the daily religious service on board. His colleagues were not likely to doubt his word. The Welsh claimed that he had wriggled forward after the tackle had been made, which was why Morgan was holding onto him. Referee Dallas, who had slipped all afternoon as he chased play because he was wearing regular formal shoes, was in Kiwi eyes too far away to make an accurate call. The members of the press, half a pitch away and struggling to make out the action through the poor afternoon light were also too far away to make any definitive statements – not that it stopped them speculating. Quite how the boys in the trees managed to convey all this to the anxious, sore-necked folk down below we can only guess. The 'no try' decision was the main talking point back in New Zealand for years to come, which is a pity, as most observers noted that the Welsh fully deserved to win on the day.

At the final whistle, Gallaher and Nicholls exchanged their shirts and shook hands before a procession bore 'Prince Gwyn' away. Carriages swept the exhausted players off to the after-match function at the Esplanade in Penarth, and the trains home to the valleys were running late into the night conveying thousands of happy Welsh fans. Never have three points been so lavishly celebrated.

Just a week after history was made at Cardiff, the Originals had to face Charlie once more, this time as skipper of a confident Newport side. The home team was roared on by a full house of 12,000 at Rodney Parade, the biggest crowd at the stadium since England had played Wales there in 1897. Low temperatures had led to the ground staff covering the pitch in straw, and the last few wisps were stirred up as Charlie's side faced the Haka. The Rodney Parade faithful responded with a passionate rendition of 'Hen Wlad fy Nhadau' – just a week after Cardiff, the hymn had become embedded in Welsh rugby's soul.

It was always destined to be a tight match. A tough, resilient Newport outfit, proud of its reputation as one of Welsh rugby's giants, was keen to measure itself against the touring side. The Originals would have been rocked by the unfamiliar experience of being on the losing side at Cardiff. The long tour was certainly taking its toll, and they were without their own inspirational captain again at Rodney Parade, but nevertheless they knew that their place in history depended on a bounce back to form. In rugby terms,

Wales was no place for a touring party to run out of steam. Inside the next week, they would have to go on to play Cardiff and Swansea. It was an itinerary that would destroy modern players – and their physios. Newport had welcomed back Charlie's cousin, Cliff Pritchard, who now played his club rugby at Pontypool. He would have been confident after showing up well against the All Blacks at Cardiff, but early exchanges showed that the tourists were in a determined mood. Cliff and the Newport midfield were faced with some ferocious tackling, and then split apart by a clever counter attack that led to a try by Eric Harper. Then, just as Charlie's pack started to exert some pressure, and appeared to be gaining the upper hand, Billy 'Carbine' Wallace kicked a long penalty goal to double their lead.

The resulting six-point margin was bound to a decisive one in such a close match. A second half penalty by full-back Griffiths closed the gap, and both sides were, like exhausted prize fighters, still slugging it out right up to the bell. Charlie's dream of defeating the All Blacks twice in a week was over, however Newport were establishing a proud tradition against touring sides, and the fact that his side had run the All Blacks closer than Scotland, Ireland or England would have rung hollow in the home dressing room after the game.

The All Blacks continued to show their mettle during their remaining tour matches in Wales. Cardiff were denied a famous victory by 10 points to 8 on Boxing Day, and a freakishly long drop goal off 'Carbine' Wallace's 'weaker' left foot meant that the All Whites of Swansea were defeated by the All Blacks by 4 points to 3. By the time the Originals boarded the ship for France in Southampton, it was clear that the tour had been defined by the Welsh leg of the tour. They had only conceded seven tries in the whole tour, and four of those had been against Welsh teams. As they walked up the gangplank at Southampton docks, a group of Welsh students from the city's university sang 'Sosban Fach'. For both rugby nations, this tour had done much to define who they were.

After the dust had settled on the 1905-06 season, Newport's

scrum-half Tommy Vile reflected on the impact of the Originals on Welsh rugby. He admired their ability to play according to the conditions, showing an ability to switch their approach from free-flowing attack to hard-nosed defence. Vile was, as his biographer Philip Grant says, a 'Giant of a Man', a diminutive but brave player with a huge rugby brain. He was destined to succeed Charlie as captain of the Black and Ambers, and has to be regarded as very unlucky not to have been playing on that historic day in Cardiff on the 16 December 1905. As with countless other unrecognised sporting talents, it was Vile's misfortune to be up against one of the game's greats, Swansea's Dickie Owen. His clever reverse pass from the base of the scrum had unlocked the All Black defence for Teddy Morgan's try, but there were many commentators and players who felt that by 1905 Vile was the superior all round player. His forensic analysis of the 1905 Originals pinpoints the fact that it was the Wellington scrum-half Fred Roberts who failed to capitalise on a rare break in the second half that could have levelled the score. Roberts was generally acknowledged to be one of the stars of this All Black side. He was certainly one of the touring party's biggest personalities. At a mid-voyage stop at Tenerife, it was Roberts who rounded up some local street traders and persuaded them to operate as opposition for some lineout practice on the beach. The renowned Kiwi rugby writer and broadcaster Winston McCarthy described Roberts as 'a superb passer, a judicious runner from the scrum, and excellent two-footed kicker and a giant on defence.' The fact that he had to play 28 of the 32 games on the 1905 tour may have had some bearing on the relative dip in form. There is no doubt, however, that the relentless pressure put on him by Charlie and the Welsh pack was the main reason why the Wellington man was a percentage point or two off his best. The tour ended disastrously for Roberts. On the North American return leg of the journey, he fell ill, and a surgeon on the West Coast decided to take out Fred's tonsils without anaesthetic. Clearly unfit to travel any further, it was his close friend 'Carbine' Wallace who volunteered to stay behind with him.

Happily, Roberts made a full recovery, and went on to captain the All Blacks in his final tour to Australia in 1910.

For Tommy Vile – and countless others – the star of the touring side was the irrepressible 'Carbine' Wallace. 'First among them I would place WJ Wallace, a man with a quite exceptional brain. As an all-round footballer Wallace was one of the best men I have ever seen.' Wallace scored 246 points on the tour, a record that still stands today. OL Owen, writing for *The Times*, reminisced in 1960 and reflected thus: 'To me he remains the most wonderful back ever …'

Charlie would have been pleased to secure the shirt of Frank Glasgow after the match. The Taranaki forward was adjudged one of the successes of the tour, playing in 27 of the 35 matches, and appearing in all five international games. His points tally of eight tries, five conversions and a penalty goal made him the leading scorer amongst the forwards. The All Black seven on that December afternoon in Cardiff was a formidable opponent – tough, clever and athletic. It is equally possible that it was Frank who sought out Charlie Pritchard after the final whistle, the sporting gesture of a rugby man who knew he had met his match. For all the brilliance of 'Prince Gwyn' and his backs, the Welsh win highlighted what any rugby player knows – that the game is won and lost in the forwards. A fierce competitor like Glasgow would have recognised that it was Charlie's performance that gave the Welsh pack the edge on that day.

SOUTH AFRICA

'We agreed to call ourselves Springboks ...'
Paul Roos

The extravagantly moustachioed face of the skipper of the touring South African side of 1906 became a familiar one in South Wales. A deeply religious man, Roos had turned down an opportunity to play in the Currie Cup back home on account of the fact that it necessitated travel on the Sabbath. When he arrived in South Wales he took to the pulpits of the Valleys to spread the Gospel. He would have been aware that the crusading preacher Evan Roberts had trodden the same path in previous years, and a Revivalist movement had taken root in some communities. Rugby had been in Roberts' sights. Like Roos, he was against playing sport on the Sabbath, and attacked the drinking that was (allegedly) associated with rugby clubs. He had some success – rugby convert Jenkin Thomas famously exclaimed, 'I used to play full-back for the devil, but now I am forward for God'. Some rugby clubs heeded the call, and teams turned up to chapel instead. By 1906, however, some of the steam had gone out of the Revivalist movement. Gareth Williams, writing in *Fields of Praise*, feels that the Wales victory of 1905 against the All Blacks did much to blunt the advance of the Revivalists. Rugby, he said, was now able to take on a quasi-religious role, becoming the 'popular mass activity' of choice. When we hear hymns belted out at the Principality Stadium in Cardiff, we are listening to the dying throes of popular religion, rather than evidence of its enduring power. Welsh rugby would have had much to fear from a popular, respected rugby man like Roos touring the pulpits a year or two before the arrival of the South Africans in 1906. As it was, he did his damage on the pitch.

In rugby terms, contact with South Africa began in 1891 with the arrival of a British touring side. As rugby 'missionaries', they had been financed by the arch colonialist Cecil Rhodes. Twenty games were played and won, and only a point conceded. Five years later, the South Africans won the last Test in a four-game series, and the rapid development of the game in South Africa was clear. Their captain 'Fairy' Heatlie borrowed some kit from his own club, Old Diocesans, and the distinctive dark green shirts became part of South Africa's rugby image. After the Boer War, rugby became one of the obvious ways for both sides to repair the damage, and another British touring side arrived in 1903. By this time, pupil had turned master, and the South Africans won the series. Indeed, they would not lose another Test series – at home, or away – until 1956.

Acutely aware of the importance of the 1906 tour, team manager Cecil Carden had convened a rapid meeting with captain Paul Roos and his vice-captain, Paddy Carolin. Carden told them that he felt that the side needed to get its PR right – a remarkably modern piece of thinking. He feared that 'the witty London press would invent some funny name for us if we did not invent one for ourselves.' A look at the granite South African faces on the 1906 team photograph might suggest that these visitors from the Southern Hemisphere would be unlikely to have their feelings hurt by some name-calling, but nevertheless Carden's insight had allowed Roos to get ahead of the press. When he was asked the question at a news conference, he was able to get the name 'Springboks' into the papers, and into rugby lore. Throughout the tour, in chatting to the press, to congregations at churches and at post-match dinners, Roos proved to be an inspired choice as captain. Always striking the right note, he was able to handle the off-field demands of the job without letting it affect his form in the matches. The players themselves had voted for him, and this would have given him some degree of confidence. They all knew that it was a huge responsibility.

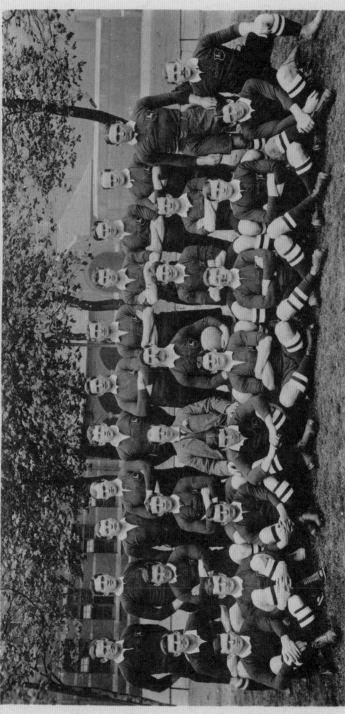

A. F. W. MARSBERG, A. STEGMANN, A. F. BURDETT, W. MORKEL, H. G. REID, J. W. S. RAAF, D. J. BRINK, H. J. DANEEL, J. LE ROUX, J. A. LOUBSER, H. A. DE VILLIERS,

H. W. CAROLIN, W. A. BURGER, W. C. MARTHEZE, J. C. CARDIN, MANAGER. P. J. ROOS, CAPTAIN. J. LE ROUX, H. A. DE VILLIERS, S. MORKEL, D. S. MARE,

THE SOUTH AFRICAN RUGBY FOOTBALL TEAM.
THE "SPRINGBOKS."

F. S. DOBBIN, W. A. NEILL, S. C. DE MELKER, W. A. MILLAR, P. A. LE ROUX, A. R. BURMEISTER, D. C. JACKSON, J. G. HIRSCH.

COPYRIGHT.

Davidson Brothers
LONDON.

When he was elected, Roos got to his feet and said 'I would like to make absolutely clear at the outset we are not English-speaking or Afrikaans-speaking, but a band of happy South Africans.' From the very outset, South African rugby was being played in the eye of political storms. Roos was leading a touring side that would have been split between Boers and Colonials in a bitter war that had only ended four years previously. They were going to tour Britain – the colonial power that had aimed to subdue the Boer farmers, setting up concentration camps to incarcerate their families in the process. Some 28,000 Boer women and children had died in those camps, as well as at least 20,000 Black South Africans. One of the star Springboks, Sammy Morkel, had fought at the Battle of Paardeberg, and had been imprisoned afterwards. It was a testament to Roos' leadership that he should take on this responsibility and emerge from the experience as the hugely respected player and captain of a highly successful side. His team-mates had chosen well.

Predictably, the tour itinerary was brutal. There were to be 29 matches, including Tests against the four home nations, and a fixture against the emerging French in Paris. Following hot on the heels of Dave Gallaher's Originals, Roos and his team were bound to be compared to the 1905 tourists. Despite team manager Carden's PR savvy, and Roos' studied diplomacy, the early match against Devon on the 17 October 1906 drew some unwelcome publicity. The Springboks were faced with the selection of James Peters. As the first black rugby player to play for England, Peters was no stranger to controversy. Some of Roos' squad refused to take the field to play a 'savage', and the authorities had to call in the South African High Commissioner to talk to the squad. A riot seemed likely on the packed terraces. It is unlikely that any of this fazed Peters, who had been brought up in a circus troupe and had seen his father mauled to death by a lion. Abandoned by his mother, Peters had picked up the sport at a home for orphans. What pleasantries he exchanged with the tourists when they finally came out to face the men from Devon is not recorded.

The four-try Springbok victory of 22-6 over Devon was overshadowed by the Peters controversy, which foreshadowed the issue of apartheid that did so much to damage the Springbok brand in the second half of the century. Rugby was, of course, a white man's game in South Africa. It was not until 1981 that the gifted Errol Tobias managed to become the first black rugby player to don the green Springbok shirt.

As with the All Blacks of 1905, however, Roos' side began putting the clubs and counties of England to the sword with their brand of powerful attacking rugby. Their physically imposing backs ran hard and fast at opposing defences, with a tough, athletic set of forwards providing plenty of possession. A close match against Glamorgan suggested that Wales would be the big threat for the tourists, but defeat came to the South Africans in the form of the Scots. A shoulder injury sustained in the match against Oxford University had sidelined the skipper, and two second half tries put an end to the Springboks' winning run. An impressive crowd of 30,000 at Hampden Park saw the tourists' flow of ball interrupted by the sticky ground conditions and the feisty Scottish forwards. Tries by MacLeod and Purves saw the home side close out the game at 6-0.

Across the Irish Sea at the Balmoral Showgrounds, Roos' patched up shoulder allowed him to lead his team into the Test against Ireland. His team seemed to have recovered their composure after the Scottish match, and they moved through the gears smoothly enough to get to half-time 12-3 up. The faster ground was to their liking, and two tries by Loubser and another by Krige put the tourists in control. Whatever was dispensed to the Irish at half-time – wisdom, tactical insight or tea cups smashed against walls – the second half turned out to be a classic. The game was levelled at 12-12 before an excruciatingly late Springbok score by Stegmann decided what had become an epic contest.

The close match against Glamorgan earlier in the tour had reinforced the belief that the Welsh leg of the tour would be the acid test for Roos' men. Wales were, on paper, a huge threat. They were at the very pinnacle of the game, having defeated the All Blacks in an unofficial World Championship decider in December of 1905. They had been the dominant home nation side in the opening years of the twentieth century. The game against Newport, led by Charlie Pritchard, would be a searching examination of their skills. Roos' vice-captain Paddy Carolin soaked up the Welsh rugby vibe. In a letter home he wrote 'Wales is a veritable hotbed of rugby football and no wonder Welshmen play it as they do when every man in Wales holds such a high opinion of the men who play and win such laurels for their Principality.'

When the Springboks arrived at Rodney Parade they were expecting a tough encounter. Charlie Pritchard's men were in a good vein of form, having won their opening four fixtures of the season, and had been unlucky to go down 3-0 to the Old Enemy, Cardiff. Charlie was the beating heart of a pack that contained Black and Amber luminaries such as Hodges, Boots and Jenkins. The half-backs Vile and Martin were as potent a combination as the Springboks were likely to encounter. A good crowd of 18,000 backed up the Newport Town Band in belting out a rousing version of 'Hen Wlad fy Nhadau', and Charlie took the kick-off.

Afterwards Carolin admitted that he was relieved to have won the game. The Newport forwards, led by Pritchard, were 'cleverer and more vigorous' than the South African pack, and dominated the early exchanges. As the Springboks gained a foothold in the game, they began to stretch the Newport defence with swift, accurate passing. Out in the backs Stegmann was a constant threat, and soon he broke clear to score the game's opening try. Another smart passing move gave him his second score, and the Springboks were 8-0 up. In such a tightly contested match, this was always going to be enough. Frustratingly for the crowd, the Newport backs fumbled a gilt-edged chance just before half-time. The second half was more of the same. Charlie's pack were getting the best of the set piece exchanges, but the Springbok full-back Marsberg dealt majestically with the tactical kicking game of Vile and Martin. The Newport forwards were repeatedly having to trot back into their own half after gaining possession, a disheartening feeling for any side. A strong home attack looked destined to bring them a deserved score, but Thomas was bundled into touch five yards short of the line. Marsberg then pulled off an excellent tackle on the same player when he was just ten yards out after Gunstone had freed him from the shackles of the Springbok defence. Charlie's side, for all his efforts, failed to score, and the Springboks rolled on.

In the wake of the game, Roos and Pritchard sat down over a drink to discuss the game. Reportedly, Roos asked how the Newport forwards had managed to dominate possession. Despite being on the losing side, the Black and Amber pack had been acknowledged to have won their own private battles that day, and the sportsmanlike Pritchard openly discussed their approach to the set piece. When Roos shook his hand on the platform at Newport station the following morning, the affable Pritchard was not to know that a 'Welsh Plan' was already taking shape. It is a matter of some debate as to whether this plan was the decisive factor in the eventual defeat of Wales. The letters of vice-captain Paddy Carolin seem to suggest that the Springboks learned nothing new from their outing at Rodney Parade. Pritchard would have explained that the disruption of the feed of the ball into the Springbok scrum was calculated to encourage the half-back to try the other side – hence Newport would 'win the loose-head'. This came as no shock to the tourists, who had done their homework on the Welsh pack. The match against the Black and Ambers would have sharpened their focus in this respect, but first the tourists' mazy itinerary was to take them back across the Severn.

In the run-up to the Welsh game, Gwyn Nicholls was coaxed out of his self-imposed international retirement to have 'a shot at the Springboks'. Would this be a game too far for the Prince of Centres? The pundits made the home team hot favourites after their defeat of the All Blacks. Carolin, writing from the genteel surroundings of the Hotel Metropole in Swansea, was happy with the underdog tag. 'They will find us harder opponents than they anticipate,' he wrote.

As it transpired, the game was a huge disappointment for everyone but the Springboks. The twin threat of Gabe and Nicholls in the centre was snuffed out by the hard-nosed Springbok defence, and Roos' cordial chat with Charlie at Rodney Parade meant that his forwards got the better of the arm wrestle up front. 'Our backs had a real field day' wrote a triumphant Carolin. 'It is no exaggeration to say that never for five consecutive minutes did they look like a winning side'. The 'Welsh Plan' had worked, and it was a damning indictment of the Welsh performance on the day. The *Daily Mail* commented that the Springboks had excelled where the New Zealanders had failed. The 11-0 victory was a sizeable feather in the touring team's hat. After the match, the knowledgeable Welsh crowd had helped to chair Roos and his star player, full-back Arthur Marsberg, the 'Lion of the Plains', from the field. Roos said later that it was one of the proudest moments of his life. The defeat ended the international careers of several Welsh players – including 'Prince Gwyn'. He was injured (and probably too heart-sick) to deliver the post-match dinner speech, and Charlie stood in for his skipper. It may well be that this is where he was presented with the shirt that now graces the Pritchard Collection.

The Springboks crossed the border once more, travelling to meet England at a depressingly wet Crystal Palace. Both sides struggled in the conditions, with the cloying mud and the slippery ball making coherent rugby all but impossible. The afternoon ended on a 3-3 draw, with both sets of players exhausted and all but unrecognisable.

The last leg of the tour took Roos and his men back into Wales – it is interesting to note that even a hundred years ago, touring itineraries were being put together with all the logic of a drunk man in a wine cellar. The Springboks kept their sense of momentum going, defeating a strong Monmouthshire side back at Rodney Parade and then subduing Llanelli. Their final game before crossing the Channel to France was against Cardiff, captained by the mercurial Percy Bush. Gwyn Nicholls, who had taken much of the flak from the Welsh press in the wake of the Welsh defeat at St Helen's, lined up in the centre. Surprisingly, Roos' side ended this final leg of the tour on a low. Although they were prepared for the game as meticulously as ever – the announcement that Cardiff were going to field three half-backs in the form of Bush, Morgan and Gibbs resulted in a detailed team meeting and a discussion on tactics – they were defeated by four tries to nil by a Cardiff side bristling with intent, and perhaps determined to salvage some Welsh pride. Bush's men were sharper on the day, adapting to the conditions by kicking in behind the Springbok forwards, and defending resolutely against the big Springbok runners. The highlight of this game, fought out in such difficult conditions, was a try by the newly capped Welsh flyer Johnny Williams. He had played at Newport with Charlie, who would have been delighted to see the Whitchurch boy make his debut against the Springboks, albeit as a Cardiff player. After a quiet debut in the red shirt of Wales, he shocked the Springboks by swerving his way round Marsberg to score. The 'Lion of the Plains', whose tacking on tour had drawn gasps of astonishment from the crowds, had been completely outfoxed. It was typical of the man that he should trot back to shake Johnny's hand after the try was scored. Williams went on to a dazzling international career, only losing twice in a Welsh shirt. Tragically, he was one of the 4,000 Welshmen killed or wounded in the muddy crossfire and confusion of the attack at Mametz Wood on the Somme in July 1916.

It was a deeply satisfying return to form for Gwyn Nicholls, who dominated the midfield exchanges. The ever-diplomatic Roos acknowledged as much in his post-match speech, when he confessed that 'It is only human to be disappointed in having been beaten … but I am glad for one man's sake that you had such a glorious success, and that is our friend Gwyn Nicholls …'

In the challenging role of tour skipper, Paul Roos played a blinder from start to finish. His side had in technical terms given the established northern hemisphere teams a prolonged lesson in how to play the game. They had championed the 3-4-1 formation in the scrum, the template that was to go on to prove the standard formation. Their running and passing under pressure was at least the equal of the triumphant All Blacks of 1905. Newport's Tommy Vile, writing in the wake of the tour, was impressed by their approach.

'They were learning all the time,' said the diminutive half-back and future International referee. In that respect, he felt they were more impressive than the All Blacks of 1905, who Vile felt had a system that they stuck to rigidly.

Roos' Original Springboks played 28 games in Britain, winning 25, drawing one and losing just two. They scored 553 points and conceded only 79. But as with Dave Gallaher's side, the statistics tell only a fraction of the story. As with the New Zealanders, the tour had made a statement on behalf of an emerging nation, as powerful and far-reaching as that moment when another Springbok skipper shook hands with his president at the Rugby World Cup Final in 1995. When asked about the impact of the 1906 tour, Roos managed to find the right words again.

'The tour has united us from Cape Agulhas to the Zambesi. South Africa was one, and all the differences had been forgotten. Here, we are one; may it always be the same.'

The victory of the 2019 Springbok side at the Rugby World Cup in Japan prompted similar sentiments. It is interesting how in 1906, 1995 and 2019 rugby is seen as a unifying factor. Siya Kolisi, South Africa's first ever black captain, took on the role performed by Paul Roos and Francois Pienaar. It seems unfair to judge a rugby player through a political prism, but sportsmen in that country have had to live with a difficult and divisive legacy in the past century.

AUSTRALIA

AUSTRALIA

'Alone of all the races on earth, they seem to be free from the "Grass is greener on the other side of the fence" syndrome, and roundly proclaim that Australia is, in fact, the other side of the fence.'

Douglas Adams

At the cemetery in the sleepy town of Maitland in rural New South Wales there is a proud white stone memorial to an English rugby player. The inscription at the base reads:
'By kindly hands thy humble grave adorned
By strangers honoured and by strangers mourned'.

RL Seddon was a Lancastrian, a forward who played his club rugby at Swinton. At the age of twenty-eight he was drowned when his boat overturned on the Hunter River. The *Otago Witness* said that Seddon had been 'indulging in a little sculling exercise'. A letter recovered from his pocket described how he and his friends had been on a kangaroo hunting expedition just a few days previously, and that he was looking forward to some more leisure time on the river. Seddon was taking it easy in the middle of a busy itinerary that was taking his group all round Australia. The behaviour of some tourists in his party had caused a stir, with a local paper outraged by 'three galoots' who 'invaded a first-class carriage' on one of the many journeys the team had to make. The unnamed threesome proceeded to 'guzzle tea without paying'. The tour had been organised by two prominent Victorian sporting icons, Arthur Shrewsbury and Alfred

Shaw. Despite operating as a private venture, this 1888 expedition is generally acknowledged to be the very first British Lions outing. Seddon was its captain.

The sport was rooted in Australian soil long before Seddon's rugby missionaries started to terrorise first class carriages. Indeed, there is a reference in a Sydney newspaper as far back as 1829 to off duty soldiers at the town's barracks being 'in the habit of amusing themselves with the game of football'. The correspondent went on to explain to his readership that this game was 'much played in Leicestershire'. Bearing in mind that the establishment of the Leicester Tigers was still fifty-one years away, it may be that this particular news hound had assumed that the town of Rugby was in Leicestershire, rather than Warwickshire. Besides, he may have decided, who was going to travel ten thousand miles or more to check? As the nineteenth century wore on, 'football' spread beyond the confines of the Sydney Barracks, and was seen as a suitable winter game to keep athletes fit for the cricket season. From the very start, Australian rugby union had to fight for its place in the sporting pecking order. Back in London, the RFU saw tours Down Under as an ideal way to give the sport a 'leg up'.

From the very outset, even before a drop of tea was guzzled, the 1888 tour was beset by controversy. Halifax's Jack Clowes admitted that he had been paid £15 as a clothing allowance, and when the RFU heard this news he was banned from playing. By that stage, however, Clowes was on the boat to Australia. Arthur Shrewsbury was not perturbed, reassuring his partner Shaw that Clowes was 'a dead head and of no use to us at all'. The Clowes affair set the tone for over a century of amateur Lions tours, when players were forced to leave their jobs and homes for months on end to allow them to play in that most special of teams. The bald assumption was that rugby union players could afford to do so. Charlie Pritchard may have been considered for the Anglo-Welsh tour of 1908, but a young family and increased responsibility in the family firm would have made it difficult to contemplate, quite apart from his growing injury concerns.

The RFU had sanctioned the 1888 expedition on the strict

understanding that the principle of amateurism was upheld. It may well be that Shrewsbury and Shaw underestimated the RFU's serious intent on the matter, as it is generally acknowledged that the whole party would have received the same clothing allowance as Clowes, if not more besides. 'Shamateurism' was born, and in under a decade it had ripped English rugby apart.

Despite the obvious danger that money would change hands, the tour offered the RFU a great opportunity to spread the rugby gospel. For some, tours represented an overt example of the game being utilised as a means of strengthening the bonds of Empire. In the case of Australia, rugby union has always had to fight the good fight against both rugby league and Australian Rules football. Union, with its links to the English public schools, was looked upon with some suspicion by some Australians. The increasingly independent-minded citizens of the Empire needed some persuasion to take part in a game that was so rigidly controlled from London.

Two rugby union bodies were eventually established – the Southern Rugby Union of New South Wales and the Northern Rugby Union of Queensland. These two organisations managed to put together a representative side in June 1899 to play another British Isles side, this time captained by Matthew Mullineux. Starring a young Cardiff centre called Gwyn Nicholls, the 1899 side was the first truly British touring side. Much to their surprise, these visiting rugby missionaries were beaten 13-3 by the Australians in the first Test. The following Tests were won by the visitors, but Australian rugby union was now on the world sporting map. They still lacked unity, playing in pale blue jerseys when they were in New South Wales, and donning the Queensland maroon for their game in Brisbane, but their skill and competitive edge had made an impression.

In 1903 Australian rugby players faced a Haka for the very first time as they met the All Blacks at the Sydney Cricket Ground. The excellent conditions made for a fast game, and the New Zealanders ran in three tries, all backed up by the accurate boot of 'Carbine' Wallace. The 22-3 victory for the visitors was the start of one of the game's great rivalries.

In 1904, the RFU sent another boatload of sporting missionaries Down Under, this time under the leadership of the fearsome Scottish forward David Bedell-Sivright. In a match against the Northern Districts at Newcastle, New South Wales, Oxford University's Denys Dobson entered the history books as the first overseas rugby tourist to be sent off. Dobson was a popular member of the squad, and he played in all four of the Tests on the tour. When he contested a decision by referee Harry Dolan after a scrum infringement, his choice of language led to the official sending him off. Exactly what was said was hotly disputed at the time and in subsequent inquiries. Bedell-Sivright led the rest of the Lions from the field, only emerging some twenty minutes later after some heated discussions. Dobson remained off the park for the rest of the game. In reporting the event, the rugby correspondent 'Wing Forward' said that Dobson had 'made use of an expression which is not used in polite society'. When questioned after the event, David Bevell-Sivright, no stranger to controversy himself, stood up for his team-mate, saying that he could not believe that 'one of the quietest and most gentlemanly members of the team' could be guilty of such behaviour. It may be that the Dobson affair was the culmination of some frustration that had been building up inside the touring party. Then as now, the rugby authorities faced criticism on the grounds of differing interpretations on points of rugby law. They were, it seemed, two hemispheres divided by the same sport. Dobson later served in Africa during World War 1, and his short but eventful life was brought to an end by a charging rhinoceros. 'He always did have a weak hand-off' said one of his sensitive Oxford tutors.

It is not known if Charlie was asked to tour in 1904. He certainly would have been a year later, when it was clear that he was one of Wales' core forwards. It may be that the birth of his son Cliff, and his greater responsibilities in the workings of the family wine business made a lengthy overseas tour impossible to contemplate. A postcard from Charlie to his wife survives in the family archive. 'What ho!' writes Charlie, 'I'm away from you at last.' The breezy tone might suggest that Florence Pritchard was not altogether happy with her husband's rugby jaunts around the country. Selling the idea of an extended overseas trip Down Under may have been beyond even a charmer like Charlie. Tommy Vile and Willie Llewellyn were Newport's representatives on the 1904 tour, with the latter an established star on the Welsh backline. Vile, the diminutive half-back who was the beating heart of the pre-war Black and Amber side, joined the ranks of the Lions who were capped on tour before they were capped for their country. In Tommy's case, Dickie Owen kept him out of a Welsh jersey for another four years. He went on to gain eight Welsh caps over the course of thirteen years.

In 1908, as the very first Model T Fords began to roll off the production lines in the United States, the steamship Omrah left Australia with their very first overseas touring side. As with the New Zealanders of 1905 and the South Africans of 1906, this was an emerging country's chance to make a mark in the world. Captained by a doctor, Herbert ('Paddy') Moran, they were to play an exhausting 31 games. Moran was to become a leading authority on cancer treatment when his playing days were over, but as with Gallaher and Roos before him, he would need every ounce of his diplomatic and man management skills in the weeks ahead. Just like Dave Gallaher and Paul Roos, Moran had to deal with the buzz of eager journalists all wanting to know what this latest touring side should be known as. In previous conversations, the management team had already decided against the uninspiring name of 'The Rabbits'. So it was that this latest southern hemisphere side would henceforth be known as 'The Wallabies'. A little more exotic, perhaps, and not as fluffy.

The question of living expenses for players would again be raised on this tour, and Moran later said the touring party sensed bad feeling from some within the RFU on this issue. Moran even speculated if the 'Them and Us' attitude of the English officials rankled so much with the touring players that it explained why only seven members of the 31-strong squad signed up to join the ranks when war was declared in 1914. The statistic is particularly striking when one puts it alongside a report in a Sydney newspaper that notes that 197 out of 220 regular first grade players in the city had signed

AUSTRALIAN R.F.U. 1908-1909. "(WALLABIES.)"

GRIFFEN. PRENTICE. CARROLL. McCABE. STEVINSON. CARMICHAEL.
MCKIVAT. FLANAGAN. McMURTRIE. BURGE. McCUE. MIDDLETON. SMITH. RICHARDS. ROW. CRAIG.
PARKINSON. McKIVATT. MANDIBLE. McINTYRE. D'MORAN(4th)McMANAON(Mgr) WOOD(Vice Capt) BARNETT. HAMMOND. RUSSELL.
HICKEY. McARTHUR. DIX. DALY.

up. Could it be that a tour designed to strengthen Imperial ties actually served to loosen them?

Politically, Moran and his players were acutely aware that they were fighting for the limelight against a rugby league touring side from Australia, the Kangaroos. 'The subject was constantly before our minds,' said Moran. As British – and particularly English – rugby had fought for what it felt to be the soul of the game in 1895 as the Northern League split away from the RFU, so the Australian players and administrators were in the midst of a battle in 1908. A dispute had erupted over the injury that ended the playing and working career of Alex Burdon, who was hurt playing for New South Wales in 1907. There had been simmering resentment between the players and the authorities for some time, however. Although Burdon was left high and dry by the Metropolitan Rugby Union's decision to stop paying into a player insurance scheme, the drift to league was already discernible. The outrage at his case was understandable – union crowds were up, and as Huw Richards points out, the match income of the Union had tripled between 1902 and 1907.

Behind the scenes, the rebels plotted. Led by a famous cricketer, Victor Trumper, a businessman called James Giltinan and Harry Hoyle, a politician, a new organisation was set up. The New South Wales Rugby League claimed the notable scalp of Australia's biggest rugby star, Dally Messenger, as well as the names of 138 registered players. Although the popularity of the two codes was running neck and neck at the time both codes sent representative touring sides to the UK in 1908, the dominance of league was made inevitable when on return a challenge match was set up between the two sides. The appearance fee earned by all the players was enough to damn the union players. They were 'professionalised', and were left with no option but to go over to the 'other side'. Soon, says Richards, Australian rugby union 'retreated into an upper-middle-class ghetto'. By contrast, rugby league took on the mantle of the people's sport.

Apart from overcoming these political distractions, the medically minded Moran felt that the squad's greatest achievement was that no one in the party caught a sexually transmitted disease as a result of their energetic extra-curricular activities. Despite the skipper's concerns these 'First Wallabies' produced high tempo, skilful performances on the pitch. In this respect, the extra-curricular activities did not affect the Australian party to the same extent as it did on their 1910 tour to the USA and Canada, when the team was accommodated in university fraternity houses. This probably saved money on the tour budget, but the resultant strain placed on the physical reserves of the tourists by excess North American hospitality meant that the team lost against two California University sides and three Canadian provincial sides. Presumably the 1910 tour management's PR man would have been eternally thankful that Moran and his team had decided against calling them 'The Rabbits'.

Indeed, Moran's 1908 side showed some impressive form. They had been portrayed as less of a threat than the two other southern hemisphere touring sides, but they won many friends with their attacking brand of rugby. For such an inexperienced side, playing against entirely unfamiliar opposition in alien conditions, it is interesting to note that they lost only five times on a 31-match tour. The Wallabies scored 438 points and crossed for 104 tries, scoring, on average, at least three tries a game. Their skilful backs made a real impact. This was despite an early injury to their first choice fly-half Joshua Stevenson. The tour vice-captain and half-back Fred Wood was also causing some internal tensions. As he was also one of the selectors, Wood was complicating the process. Moran wrote afterwards that Wood was a 'great little player who never found his form in England. It used to be unpleasant for us when, in the face of this, he insisted for a long time on his own selection'. Paddy Moran also had to deal with the usual disciplinary issues that beset touring sides, and managed to keep the lid on an ugly incident at the match at Iffley Road which saw NSW forward Syd Middleton sent off. There was, in the words of an Australian correspondent, a resultant 'ferocious outburst of condemnation of our unsportsmanlike tactics' in the wake of Syd's dismissal. He had punched Roberts in a maul that followed a lineout, but his apology was later accepted, and he returned to action later in the tour. It is likely that Middleton had been targeted, as Australia's main source of lineout ball, and it is probably significant that Roberts shook hands with Syd after the game and observed that the Australian had been unlucky to have been spotted transgressing. Roberts had already played against the Wallabies at Devonport, and his language towards the newly arrived tourists had been 'of a picturesquely vigorous type', according to one correspondent. With the slate wiped clean, Syd went on to play a central role in the Wallabies pack. On returning to Australia, he became disillusioned by the drift to league, and focused on his other sport, rowing. After taking part in the 1908 Olympics as a rugby player, he went on to row in the 1912 Games. Syd became something of a folk hero, and was decorated at Gallipoli and the Somme during World War 1, and also awarded an OBE.

Syd was part of a gold-winning Australian rugby side in 1908, as the Olympic Games in London coincided with the Wallabies tour. Indeed, it proved to be the only Australian gold from the London Games. New Zealand and South Africa had turned down a chance to take part in the Games, as had the home nations. The Australians defeated 'Great Britain' (a Cornwall side) 32-3 at the White City Stadium in muddy, slippery conditions. The pitch was situated alongside a swimming pool so the ball had to be periodically fished out using long poles and mattresses were laid out along the touchline to prevent players sliding in. The *Daily Telegraph* account of the match details these tricky conditions, but goes on to say that the Wallabies were deserved winners of the gold medal. Cornwall, the English County Champions, were 'practically at full strength, but from start to finish they were outplayed. The methods by which this victory was gained were even more creditable to the winners than the completeness of the victory itself and it is only fair to the Australians to speak of their play in terms of unqualified praise … They gave a display of football which would have done credit to a Welsh international side, at its best.' High praise indeed, showing that the initial coolness towards this latest tranche of rugby tourists had been overcome. Moran, on the sideline because of an injury sustained in the run up to the Olympic matches, must take a great deal of credit for this change in attitude. The team was led by Chris McKivat, and there were two tries for St George's Daniel Carroll, who also won an Olympic rugby gold playing for the USA in 1920.

On 12 December 1908, the Wallabies played their first ever Test match on British soil at Cardiff. Moran's side had to respond to the majesty of thirty thousand voices belting out 'Hen Wlad fy Nhadau' by performing the Wallaby war cry, a PR stunt that Moran regarded as 'an affliction'. In later years, he gave vent to his feelings on the matter;

> 'The memory of that war cry provokes anger in me even after all these years ... We were expected to leap in the air and make foolish gestures which somebody thought Australian natives might have used in similar circumstances ...'

The Haka it was not, a fact underlined by the ever-mischievous Percy Bush, who responded to the Wallaby war cry by appearing on the pitch brandishing a sword. Despite this motivational own goal, the tourists went on to give the Welsh a fright, losing by only one score. The *Hobart Daily Post* described the match as 'fast and strenuous', and Moran frankly admitted afterwards that it was 'one of the hardest games I had ever played in'. He was chaired from the pitch on the shoulders of the excited Welsh fans. As proud as he would have been of that moment, he knew that the Wallabies had come very close to making history. Tries by Charles Russell and Tom Richards had put the Wallabies within touching distance of a shock victory, and the last attack of the game had fizzled out because an Australian player decided to bulldoze his way through Bert Winfield rather than looking for a pass. The ever-dependable Cardiff full-back clattered into the ball carrier, and the final whistle blew.

A week later, the Wallabies enjoyed a hard fought 5-3 win over a tough Newport side at a soaking Rodney Parade. The game was notable for its late start, as Moran sportingly agreed to a delayed kick-off to allow centre Jack Jones to make his way to the ground. He

The 1908 Wallaby war cry – skipper Paddy Moran was scathing about being asked to "leap into the air and make foolish gestures"

had missed the train from Pontypool. With Charlie injured, Tommy Vile took over the captaincy of a side that contained 10 Welsh caps, as well as a Springbok ('Birdy' Partridge) and an 'Englishman' (Stanley Williams). To win in those conditions, against such a strong club outfit, would have been a huge boost for Moran and his side. Once more, the Black and Ambers came a close second to a touring side. Newport had become one of those awkward fixtures on a touring itinerary, as the Springboks of 1912 and the All Blacks of 1963 were to discover to their cost.

With the rugby authorities in Scotland and Ireland keeping up their aloof attitude towards any rugby encounter that had the faintest whiff of filthy lucre, Moran's side were only exposed to two Test matches during the tour. The match against England was to have been played at Twickenham but bad weather had delayed the construction of the stand and the match was moved to Blackheath. As with the All Black tour three years earlier, the England selectors made the mistake of fielding an experimental side. The Wallabies made them pay the price. Ten new England caps, including an all new three-quarter line, struggled to contain the impressive Australians. England started well enough and Northampton's Edgar Mobbs scored, but when Norm Row kicked an up-and-under, followed it up and scored to level the scores the game turned. Half-time came at 3-3, but the warning signs were there. Moran's Wallabies then enjoyed the better of the second half, and 'Boxer' Russell scored the Wallabies' second and third tries. His record of 24 tries on that 1908 tour still stands as a record.

The Pritchard Collection has two pale blue Australian shirts, both sporting the red waratah flower, the state emblem of New South Wales. One has 'AUSTRALIA' stitched under the flower, and this one is more likely to be the 1908 tour jersey. The second shirt may in fact be a New South Wales jersey, perhaps brought home by a 1904 tourist like team-mate Tommy Vile, or his good friend 'Rusty' Gabe. Charlie's ongoing injury problems meant that he never faced the Wallabies, but the tour itinerary could have seen him play them on three occasions – for Wales, Newport and Monmouthshire. The

last of these fixtures did not take place because of a flooded pitch, but as club captain at Newport and as a fixture in the Welsh set-up, he would have had plenty of opportunities to meet Moran and his team-mates. The Australian rugby authorities eventually adopted the use of a green jersey to overcome any accusations of NSW bias, and create a more distinct national shirt. The more familiar gold shirt was brought in to avoid a colour clash with the Springboks as late as 1961.

A month before the match against Moran's side, Charlie was injured playing Gloucester at Kingsholm. His place in the Welsh side was taken by his Newport colleague, Philip Waller, who went on to win half a dozen caps for Wales. In 1910 Waller toured South Africa with a British Isles team, playing in three Test matches, and enjoyed the country so much that he decided to stay. Waller returned to Europe to fight in the war, like so many other first-generation emigrants, and was killed in 1917 by a stray shell behind the lines near Cambrai. He is buried next to his commanding officer, Nugent Fitzpatrick, who was killed in the same blast. Fitzpatrick's father back in South Africa then campaigned for the adoption of the two-minute silence at official remembrance ceremonies. Every time we hear the 'Last Post' sounded we should remember that the two-minute silence that follows was born of the dreadful random firing of a shell and the grief of a father. And by remembering Philip Waller and his first cap against Australia we also bear witness to the Charlie Pritchard story. Grief binds.

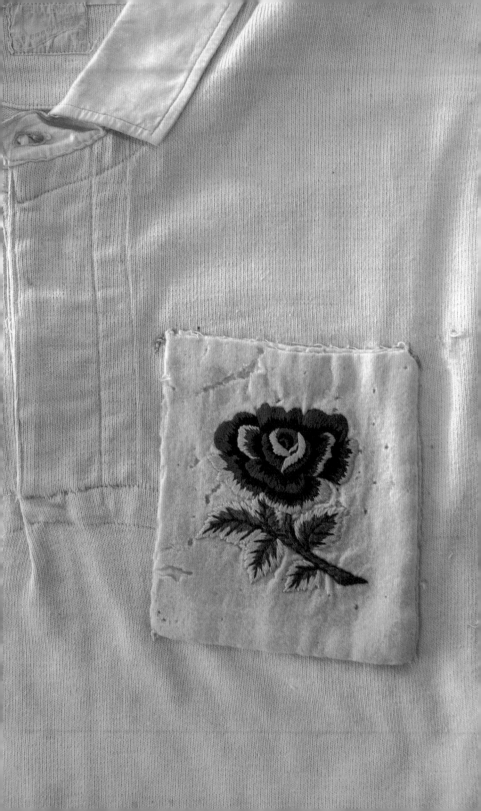

ENGLAND

'The relationship between the Welsh and the English is based on trust and understanding. They don't trust us and we don't understand them.'

Dudley Wood
(English RFU secretary on Anglo-Welsh relations, 1986.)

As Charlie Pritchard left the open arena of the new Twickenham stadium in 1910 he would have had to come to terms with the unusual sensation of being on a losing side in an England/Wales match. He had played in a winning side against the old enemy on four occasions – 1905, 1906, 1907 and 1908. In the opening moments of the match at Twickenham in 1910, however, Quins fly-half Adrian Stoop broke the shackles. Perhaps Charlie saw the writing on the wall. His knee would have been sore as he sat in the away dressing room after the match and he would have spent the afternoon pursuing players that he could imagine would be the future stars of the game – Stoop, Ronnie Poulton Palmer and Cherry Pillman. Charlie would have felt like an old man. Along with all the Welsh players, he would have been wanting to cheer up the folk in the Valleys who were going through a miners' strike. A win against the Red Rose would have lifted morale back home. In the corresponding fixture in 1906, he would have remembered, he had scored his one and only international try, and had been singing a duet with 'Rusty' Gabe on the train home to Newport. The times were a-changing.

Just as it had been a golden age for the Welsh, the start of the twentieth century had been a difficult time to be an England rugby fan. As in the 1970s, the turn of century encounters between the White and the Red shirts were on the whole not happy occasions for the England fans. The schism with the Northern League in the mid-1890s had undoubtedly deprived English rugby of a major pool of talent.

Additionally, rugbying members of His Majesty's armed forces were doing their duty overseas in China and South Africa at the turn of the century, which made it difficult for their clubs to establish a run of form. This was, of course, just as strong opposition was being developed in the other three home nations. It would have felt that English rugby was going backwards.

A key indicator of the depth of the crisis is to look at how this lack of confidence expressed itself in seemingly chaotic selection for the national side. Down in the ultra modern Home Dressing Room at Twickenham the names of all the players who have been awarded England caps are listed chronologically. The opening decade of the twentieth century has the longest list of all. At the fulcrum of the side, 16 different men played at half-back against Wales between 1899 and 1909. Jack Raphael, one of a staggeringly large group of 71 new caps handed out during this period, was not alone in suggesting that this lack of continuity betrayed a lack of vision. Gwyn Nicholls' Welsh team had a style that was widely admired, but England had 'no distinctive style of her own ... no cohesion in her play ...' Raphael's view was summarised in classic *Boys' Own* speak by the skipper of the 1903 side, Bernard Oughtred, when he said that his team had been 'beaten to blazes'.

Charlie would have heard dark mutterings of biased refereeing in the changing room before his first England game in 1905. The previous year's match had ended in a 14-14 draw at Leicester, and Wales had felt hard done by after a series of decisions culminated in a late try that had been disallowed for what was allegedly a forward pass. The ever-diplomatic captain Gwyn Nicholls refused to be drawn on the subject after the match, but the *Western Mail* did not pull any punches. 'The refereeing of Mr Findlay was extraordinary. The like of it has never been seen in Wales and there is no desire

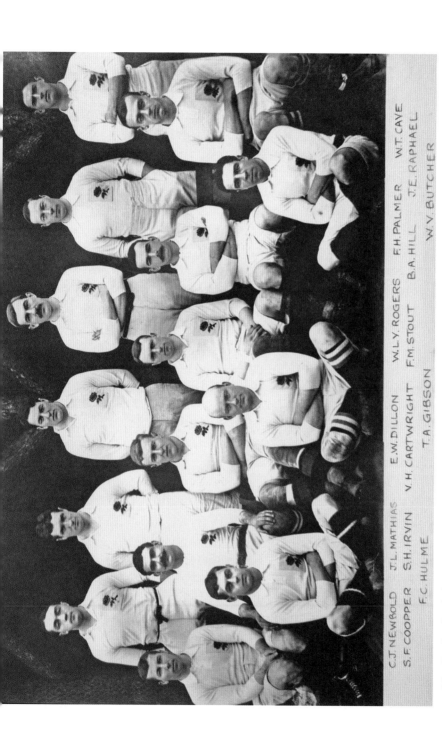

C.J. NEWBOLD   J.L. MATHIAS   E.W. DILLON   W.L.Y. ROGERS   F.H. PALMER   W.T. CAVE
S.F. COOPER   S.H. IRVIN   V.H. CARTWRIGHT   F.M. STOUT   B.A. HILL   J.E. RAPHAEL
F.C. HULME   T.A. GIBSON   W.V. BUTCHER

The England side beaten 25-0 by Wales at Cardiff 14 January 1905. It was Charlie's first game against the English.

that it ever should be seen.' During the course of the game scrum-half Dickie Owen was penalised so heavily as he fed the ball into the scrum that eventually he handed the ball over to his English opponent as a protest, and allowed him to feed the ball in. All this was a great shame, as the match was full of high speed, exciting rugby. A brace of tries by Edgar Elliot had put England's noses in front, but Welsh anger kept the contest alive until the final moments of the game. Will Joseph caught a kick in the middle of the park, and he called for the mark. Up stepped Bert Winfield, the Nottingham-born Welsh full-back. He had been rejected by the English selectors earlier in his career, and he took his revenge by nailing a huge kick to snatch a draw. Perhaps the pain felt by the RFU at this late late blow was partially responsible for Winfield's kick being the last four-pointer from the mark. The following season, it was reduced to three points.

There was more revenge in the air in 1905 to the tune of a seven-try 25-0 annihilation of a hapless England side. Charlie would have been forgiven for thinking that international rugby was easy as the Welsh pack established an early stranglehold on possession. Out in the backs, Dr Teddy Morgan scored twice, and there were tries for Willie Llewellyn, Harry Watkins, Dick Jones, Rhys Gabe and 'Boxer' Harding.

Charlie Pritchard would always remember his only international try at Richmond in 1906 against the English. Although the Red Rose forwards should have made something of their one-man advantage against the seven-man Welsh pack, they were defeated by the superior cohesion and technique of Charlie and his team-mates. Twyber Travers was now being played as a specialist hooker, packing down with Will Joseph and Jehoida Hodges in a tough front row, and benefitting from the power of the 'Boxer' Harding/Dai Jones combination behind them. The modern scrum specialisms were beginning to emerge, and it was clear that Wales were ahead of the English at this stage. The jury was still out on the roving role played by Cliff Pritchard, however. There was a fear that this was tending to clog up the midfield, stifling creativity.

The Observer admired what it called the 'leisurely excellence' of the Welsh backs. Unfortunately for the English defence, the imperious Gwyn Nicholls could only be stifled for so long. In the best moment of the match one correspondent described how he set up a Welsh try: 'The Cardiff centre beguiled the English three-quarters Hind and Raphael with a swerving run and drew the full-back Jackett before sending his wing clear.' Rugby purists have a special place in their hearts for tries that are created when the opposition is 'beguiled' rather than just 'smashed'.

The 1907 clash between the old enemies at Swansea was disrupted at the outset as the Devonport dockyard worker James Peters, England's first black player, was refused access to the England bench by an overzealous policeman. Sad to note, it was one of many such moments in his career – the touring Springboks of 1906 side had objected to being on the same pitch as Peters. In the event, England's performance was lambasted in the press as 'woefully weak' as they struggled to get to grips with the Welsh attacks. Only 12,000 turned up to see local boy Billy Trew's surgical dismantling of the English lines of defence. The Swansea public were perhaps put off by the disappointing defeat of Wales by the Springboks earlier in the season. The authorities may also have feared that England's scalp was not so highly prized. Things would change.

At Bristol's Ashton Gate on 18 January 1908 Newport's Tommy Vile finally made his international debut. It was well overdue according to many observers, who detected the fact that Dickie Owen was now beginning to lose some of his customary 'zip'. Charlie would have been delighted to see Vile pulling on the red shirt – he was his vice-captain at Rodney Parade, and destined to be one of the great Black and Amber captains when Charlie's troublesome knee injuries finally called his career to a halt. Vile would have been a worried man as the fog descended on Ashton Gate. A cancellation might well mean that Dickie Owen's injury would have cleared up in time for the re-arranged fixture. The authorities decided to play on regardless, and the match was dubbed the 'phantom football match'. With visibility down to thirty yards at kick off, Percy Bush announced to the assembled press that Wales would play 'with the fog' in the first half. In truth, the conditions gave a practical joker like Bush ample scope to have some fun. He created a break for Rusty Gabe by passing to the Cardiff centre on his left then running to his right, calling to the befuddled Englishmen as he ran. Rugby writer John Billot always admired Bush's 'incomparable individualism'. No doubt the chasing English forwards would have had something to say about that 'individualism'. It's certainly the case that Wales didn't always make the most of Bush's talents during this period, but some would suggest that Bush was guilty of the same crime.

Meanwhile, visibility was down to twenty yards, and *The Times* described how 'both fifteens frequently disappeared from sight'. Somewhere in the fog, England were in fact playing their part in a nine-try thriller. Although the Welsh had established an early buffer zone with a twelve-point lead, the English fought back through tries by Birkett, Lapage and Williamson. The England kicker that day was Bristol's Geoffrey Roberts, who was making his third and last appearance in an England shirt. A lawyer by trade who went on to be a prosecutor at the Nuremberg War Trials, Roberts would have wondered how the selectors had seen enough of the game to form the opinion that he should be dropped.

England sides struggled to make much of an impression against the great touring sides during this period. The all-conquering All Blacks gave the English defence a torrid time in December 1905. The Wallabies, playing at Blackheath's Rectory Fields in 1909, also made England look second best. The glutinous mud at Crystal Palace in December 1906 did enough to slow down the free running Springboks, and the players slogged their way to a 3-3 draw. It is significant to note that only four members of the side that played Dave Gallaher's All Blacks were facing the Springboks just a year later. By the time the Australians visited these shores Jackett, Shewring, Cartwright and Hill were also gone.

Nevertheless, the sold-out Tests against New Zealand and South Africa at Crystal Palace had seen the RFU realise the benefit of owning their own ground, a move that the Scots had already made

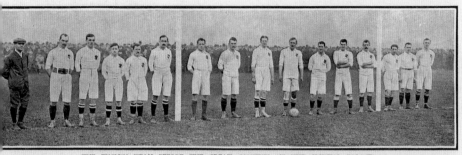

THE ENGLISH TEAM BEFORE THE GREAT CONTEST AT THE CRYSTAL PALACE

Photographed at Sydenham, December 2, 1905, by Russell

The English team was as follows: E. J. Jackett (Cornwall and Leicester), back; H. Imrie (Durham), A. E. Hind (Leicester), R. E. Godfray (Richmond), J. E. Raphael (Old Merchant Taylors'), and H. Shewring (Bristol), three-quarter backs; J. Braithwaite (Leicester) and D. Gent (Gloucester), half-backs; V. H. Cartwright (Nottingham), B. A. Hill (Blackheath), C. E. L. Hammond (Harlequins), J. L. Mathias (Bristol), E. W. Roberts (Devon), R. F. Russell (Leicester), and G. Summerscales (Durham), forwards

THE VICTORIOUS NEW ZEALAND RUGBY TEAM AT THE CRYSTAL PALACE

Photographed at Sydenham, December 2, 1905, by Russell

The team on Saturday was as follows: G. Gillett, back; W. J. Wallace, R. G. Deans, and R. MacGregor, three-quarter backs; W. Stead and J. Hunter, five-eighths; F. Roberts, half-back; D. Gallaher, winger; S. Casey, G. Tyler, J. O'Sullivan, F. Newton, C. Seeling, F. Glasgow, and A. MacDonald, forwards

The State of the English Team

The white suits of the English team became covered with mud as the play proceeded

Russell

The Scrum Break Away

The New Zealanders wore large numbers on their backs, which enabled the spectators to easily identify them

with some success with the development of the ground at Inverleith. Committee members William Williams and William Cail suggested that the RFU purchase a ten-acre site in Twickenham in 1907 for just over £5,500. The first stands were constructed the following year. Before the ground was purchased, it was used to grow fruit and vegetables, and so Twickenham Stadium was always affectionately known as the 'Cabbage Patch'. The first game to be played on the ground was a club encounter between Harlequins and Richmond in October 1909. The England v Wales game in January 1910 was the stadium's first international fixture. At this time, Twickenham had a capacity of 20,000 spectators. Although the early crowds were modest at best, the gate receipts ensured that the new venture had paid for itself inside the first three years.

Having missed the whole of the 1909 international season, the England game proved to be Charlie Pritchard's international swansong. Hugely committed player that he was, Charlie would not have enjoyed the fact that it was all to end with a vibrant England side winning 11-6. From the outset, things did not go to plan. Preparations were rushed when traffic problems delayed the kick-off, and the customary team photograph was not taken. Perhaps it was the case that Charlie saw the shape of things to come as Quins fly-half Adrian Stoop caught Ben Gronow's kick-off and immediately launched an attack. This startled the Welsh defence – a return kick was the standard response, so when Stoop set off on a diagonal run the Welsh defence was caught flat-footed. Bemused and slightly incredulous, they allowed Stoop to run too far, and the English were immediately on the front foot. Swift passing and a clever cross kick from Poulton Palmer resulted in a try by right winger Fred Chapman. At last, an England style was emerging, and Wales were clearly rattled. By half-time, Redruth's Bert Solomon had scored another try, and England held an 11-3 lead. Wales regained some of their swagger in the second half, and they came close to scoring on a couple of occasions, but Stoop's attacking tactics had done the damage. England ran out winners by 11 points to 6, and the Twickenham hoodoo had settled on the Welsh. They had lost their first Home Nations Championship match in three years, and it was Charlie's only taste of defeat in five matches against the Red Rose. Wales would not win at the new home of English rugby for another twenty-three years.

Whose England shirt is in the Pritchard Collection is impossible to say. Perhaps Charlie made a beeline for the man he saw as his toughest forward opponent on the day, as was the case with the Alfred Tedford and Frank Glasgow shirts. Perhaps the shirt was the one worn by Noel Slocock in the fog at Ashton Gate in 1908. Slocock was similarly an all action player described by rugby writer EHD Sewell as a 'terror in the tight'. Like Charlie, Noel Slocock's knee problems were becoming chronic, and 1908 was to be his last season. Like Charlie, he signed up in 1914, joining the Liverpool Scottish. He died just five days before Charlie, at Guillemont, on the Somme, and his name is in amongst over 72,000 names inscribed on the walls of the Thiepval Memorial to the Missing. On balance, it is more likely that the shirt in the Collection is from the very first Twickenham international. There is no name on the collar to help us.

On the eve of the Great War, England had shaken off the disappointments of past seasons and re-established themselves as a power in the land. The shock of the 1895 schism with the northern clubs had finally been overcome. The lack of a Home Nations Championship for England between 1894 and 1908 tells its own story. Although stripped of talent from the north, players from emerging hotbeds such as Gloucester and Bristol to the west, and Coventry and Leicester in the Midlands gave the selectors more options. Crucially, these options were not wasted, as a new found confidence allowed some consistency of selection. At the core of this English side were some exceptional and innovative players. In the forwards, Charlie would have gone toe-to-toe with new cap 'Cherry' Pillman. It was he, said *The Sportsman*, who had 'contributed more to winning the match than any other single individual', closing down the space around the fringes of the scrum usually dominated by half-backs Owen and Jones, Swansea's 'Dancing Dicks'. Frighteningly quick, and possessing the innate ability to predict where the ball would go,

Pillman was responsible for defining the role of the modern flank forward. An admiring opponent once observed that Cherry 'played a game apparently invented by himself.'

At fly-half the Dutch-born Harlequin Adrian Stoop pulled the strings. His influence cannot be underestimated. Stoop may not have been the most consistent of players on the pitch, but his technical nous and willingness to experiment moved England away from what the RFU historian OL Owen called the 'stolid and immobile' England of yore. Outside Stoop in the backs was another emerging great, Ronald Poulton Palmer. This elusive three-quarter had made headlines with a stunning five-try performance in the 1909 Varsity Match. Just as the 1995 All Blacks were reminded by fax that 'rugby is a team game: all 14 of you make sure you pass the ball to Jonah', Poulton Palmer's team-mates exploited his talents to the full. His trickery and speed had already come to the notice of the English selectors, and 'RPP' was capped for his country before he gained his Blue. Like Charlie Pritchard, he was destined for the fields of Flanders, but not before he had helped himself to four tries against the hapless French in 1914. It was to be Ronnie's last opportunity to play at the international level. He played the game in the same way as he had when he was first introduced to it at the Dragon School, Oxford and was just one of 75 'Old Dragons' to fall in the war.

As the dust settled on the 1914 season, Ronnie was described by the Rugby Football Annual as 'a born leader', so it was inevitable that as a Territorial officer in the 1/4th Royal Berkshires he should be pitched into the thick of the action. He was well known by his troops, many of whom worked for him at the Huntley and Palmer factory in Reading. In fact, there were so many of his employees in uniform that his unit was known as 'The Biscuit Boys.' They knew Ronnie as a dedicated worker, a thoughtful boss who had done a great deal to improve their working conditions, and who had spent time on the shop floor to fully understand the business. As with Charlie Pritchard, he led his men by example, and they respected him for that.

En route for the front, Poulton Palmer recounts an episode in his journal that records his own last rugby match – and that of others, too.

'After lunch we moved to Nieppe and I played rugger for the South Midland Division against the 4th Division. It was an amusing game. We had opposite us players like WJ Tyrrell (Ireland captain), HJS Morton (Cambridge and England), JG Keppell (Ireland Trials), WP Hinton (Ireland full-back) and were refereed by Basil Maclear (Ireland). I had a goodish side, mostly 5th Gloucesters and we won 14-0 but they stuck it well considering their condition. It was splendid to see so many rugger players about.'

Ronnie's Biscuit Boys were moved further south into the area around Ploegsteert Wood in April 1915. From the very outset the area seemed fraught with danger. 'The atmosphere was tainted with the smell of death …' he remarked in a letter home. Because of the wet Flanders mud, trenches could only be dug down a couple of feet, and both sides had to build sandbagged defensive positions to reinforce their positions. Inevitably, this exposed the men to sniper fire. On 28 April, one of his men, a Private Giles was shot. The teenager fell back into the trench and died in Ronnie's arms. A week later, his unit was working by night at a section of the line. Ronnie was something of a DIY addict – the family's holiday home of the Isle of Wight was an ongoing project for him – so he threw himself into the task of strengthening the dugout roof with some enthusiasm. As ever, he would not ask his troops to do something he would not do – the mark of the true leader. So it was that he was hit by a sniper's bullet while he was exposed on top of the dugout, and like Giles he fell back into the trench. Accounts differ on the exact circumstances of his last few moments. His parents were told his death was instantaneous – in other words, he was dead when he fell back into the trench. Another, possibly apocryphal account describes Ronnie managing a last line – 'I shall never play at Twickenham again'– before fading away in the arms of a fellow officer. His dead body was carried back to a support area in behind the Wood called Hyde Park Corner, and he was buried a few feet away from Private Giles. Less than a week later, Ronnie's centre partner at the 1910 Twickenham match, Gloucester's Henry Berry, was killed at the disastrous Battle of Aubers Ridge, just twenty miles or so away.

A century on, Giles and Poulton Palmer still lie side by side, the private and his commanding officer. Ronnie once said that he felt that 'Rugby is too good a game to be confined to a particular class,' and would no doubt approve of Edwin Lutyens' vision that his Commonwealth War Graves Cemeteries should reflect the fact that all are equal in death. The Hyde Park cemetery at Ploegsteert, as well as the magnificent Memorial to the Missing on the other side of the road, echoes to the birdsong from the now peaceful wood. The occasional car flashes by, and the auberge next to the cemetery does a brisk trade in the holiday season. It is a corner of a foreign field that is … well, forever England.

IRELAND

'About the only certain thing concerning Irish rugby is its uncertainty.'
From 'Rugger: the Man's Game' by EHD Sewell

The English are fond of telling the rugby world that it was an English schoolboy, William Webb Ellis, who first picked up a ball and ran with it, so giving birth to our sport. In Ireland, this standard telling of the game's origins is given a slightly different slant. Webb Ellis, the Irish will tell you, grew up in a British Army base in Tipperary. The schoolboy from Rugby was just expressing his Gaelic Football instincts in that schoolyard in 1823. Rugby is actually an Irish invention, they will tell you.

By 1899, Ireland were the Triple Crown champions, and they entered the new century in a confident frame of mind. They possessed a strong, aggressive forward pack, controlled by scrum-half Louis Magee. The opening game of the new season would have been a huge disappointment when they were roundly defeated by the English and the Welsh, and only managed a draw against the Scots. The men in green had gone from Triple Crown winners to the bottom of the Championship in a year. It was, in effect, an indicator of what was to come. Heroic performances went alongside chaotic defeats.

1900 was the beginning of Wales' golden age, when they won the coveted Triple Crown six times up to 1911. By contrast, the Irish rugby journalist Edmund Van Esbeck described Ireland as 'very much the sick man of the rugby scene', and the men in green were the only home nation not to win the Triple Crown between 1900 and

1914. Indeed, they did not win the Crown again until 1948, although they did manage some spectacular victories during these years. The team was not without players of stature, and the likes of Alfred Tedford and George Hamlet in the pack caused the opposition real problems with their energy and strength.

On Charlie Pritchard's international debut in 1904 Tedford scored twice, and after the 1906 match Charlie sought the Malone man out after the game to swap shirts with him. Tedford's name is still visible in the collar of the Irish shirt in the Pritchard Collection, and the swap may well have been initiated by Charlie because of that Man of the Match performance by his adversary on his debut. Tedford played the kind of high energy, hugely committed game that Charlie aspired to.

The Belfast-born Tedford was a forward in what we would now regard to be a modern mould. Blessed with sufficient pace and handling skills to play for Ulster out in the backs, Tedford made his debut for Ireland at Welford Road against England in the spring of 1902. Making his debut alongside him was the intriguingly named forward George Hamlet. England scrapped their way to a 6-3 win, but from that point on, Tedford was ever-present, winning 23 caps for his country and scoring six tries.

Tedford was invited to tour South Africa with the British Isles squad in 1903, which was in itself a significant achievement. The fact that he should go on to be ever-present in the Test series speaks volumes for his rate of progress as a player. Although these prototype Lions suffered the shock of being beaten by the South Africans, the accounts that survive show Tedford to have been in good form during the tour. In 40 matches over previous tours, the representative British sides had been unbeaten, but that changed in 1903. The South Africans had just emerged from a bitter war against the British, and it was felt that sport might help to heal the rift. Inevitably, the South Africans would have felt that they had a point to prove, but the success of the home side in the Tests was more than a case of greater motivation. It was obvious to all that South Africa was an emerging rugby power. The team that won the decider at

Newlands formed the nucleus of the 1906 touring Springboks that was to banish forever the idea that the Colonials were still learning how to play the game. The 1903 tour was reviewed by an Otago correspondent who noted that Tedford 'never tires, and shows up at the end of a hard fought game. He is the best forward in Ireland.' He was also judged to be the best forward in the British Isles, on this showing. Considering the fact that he was playing alongside the granite-hard Scottish pairing of Morrison and Bedell-Sivright, as well as England's Frank Stout, it was an impressive tour for the Malone man.

In what became known as 'Tedford's match' on Charlie Pritchard's debut in March 1904, there was a disappointing crowd of only 3,000, the authorities having tried to ignore a fixture clash with an international football game. In a football stronghold such as Belfast, it was a costly mistake for the Irish Rugby Football Union. Ireland's home internationals were always played at various venues, from the bigger cities of Dublin and Belfast to the smaller provincial settings of Cork and Limerick. With the ownership of the Lansdowne Road stadium settled in 1906, Irish rugby had a more permanent home in what was the oldest stadium in the home nations. Those who came to the Balmoral Showground in Belfast for the Wales clash in 1904 were rewarded with a dramatic, breathless game. Tedford's performance throughout was outstanding – tireless, brave and a constant thorn in the Welsh side. There was controversy in the first half as a forward pass was not picked up by referee Findlay Crawford, a decision that was put under the post-match microscope later as Dick Jones was disallowed a try. The Irish players magnanimously agreed that the pass Jones had received had not been forward at all, and it was not to be the only time that the Welsh players would call into question the competence – or worse – of the Scottish referee.

The Irish were behind in the dying minutes of the game. By then, the players were exhausted. A litany of injuries had disrupted the match, but increased the sense of drama. Campbell Robb, the Irish winger from Queen's University, went off to get some treatment, and Joe Wallace, a forward, found himself playing on the wing as cover.

When Robb hobbled back on the pitch the Welsh were able to exploit his inability to turn and run, and 'Rusty' Gabe's score put the Welsh into a clear lead. Robb was taken off again, and Wallace returned to the wing. With only 14 men on the pitch, Tedford and the forwards somehow found another gear. The underdogs bit back.

A debut try for winger Harry Thrift followed some determined Irish attacking, and it was clear that there had been a momentum shift. The ball was moved out wide again, and Wallace found himself boxed in near touch. He launched a speculative cross kick into the Welsh half. Bert Winfield, the Cardiff full-back, made the cardinal error of allowing the ball to bounce, only to see it scooped up by Tedford. The big Malone man rumbled in under the post for his second try of the match. It was left to Cecil Parke to kick the conversion to win the match, and a man who had the nerve to win tennis titles at Wimbledon was unlikely to miss. For Tedford, the match was a career highlight. For Pritchard, it was a debut to remember.

An ankle injury meant that Charlie missed out on an immediate rematch with Tedford, but all the talk was of another Irish debutant in 1905. Basil Maclear had been in the sights for both English and Irish selectors, as he was stationed at Fermoy, County Cork, and played much of his club rugby at Bedford and Blackheath. A representative of the English committee, Sir Rowland Hill, saw Maclear score two tries at a match in Richmond and immediately decided that he was 'not good enough'. It proved to be as accurate and clear sighted a judgement as the one handed out in 1962 by a record executive who decided that a four-piece band from Liverpool was unlikely to make the big time. In itself, Hill's dismissal of the international potential of Maclear gives us an insight as to why England rugby teams struggled during the early years of the twentieth century. Inevitably, Maclear's debut was against the English. Predictably, he was outstanding, causing havoc in the English defence. It was the first of Maclear's 11 caps, and he was never on a losing side against England. Revenge smelled of red roses to the Portsmouth-born centre.

At Cork in 1905, Ireland won 17-3. Mossy Landers remembered the day years later as 'one of the greatest displays ever put up by the wearers of green'. He was the Irish full-back on that day, and had a perfect view of the carnage created by the white-gloved Maclear in the English midfield. With their collective tails up, the Irish outplayed the Scots at Inverleith. Tedford scored once more, and he was at the core of a resolute forward display.

It was perhaps inevitable that the Irish should falter just as they were getting into the home straight of a Triple Crown campaign. The truth of the matter is, however, that the Welsh side of this era were pretty formidable in away matches, but pretty near unbeatable at home. Cork's Barrack Street Brass Band had made the journey to Swansea for the Triple Crown decider, but exceptionally rough weather on the Irish Sea crossing had resulted in some of their instruments being lost overboard. It was perhaps an omen, as veteran centre Gwyn Nicholls' chop tackles snuffed out the threat of Basil Maclear in midfield. One correspondent observed that 'Maclear will probably remember Nicholls as long as the Irish centre plays football ...' *The Times* had described Maclear as 'very hard to stop', but Nicholls had played enough rugby to know that an opponent won't get very far if you take his legs away from under him. It was a defence masterclass. The Cardiff man had been poorly received as he took the field, and Tedford's team mates must have been amazed by the sight of the Welsh captain being pelted with stones from one section of the St Helen's crowd. They discovered later that Nicholls had been returned to the side at the expense of a local favourite, Frank Gordon. By that time, the damage was done, 'Prince' Gwyn had restored his reputation and the Barrack Street Band were whistling along to the songs drifting out from the bars of Swansea.

Putting the disappointment of losing the Triple Crown behind them, the Irish now looked forward to the arrival of the All Blacks. Led by an Irishman, Dave Gallaher, the Originals were sweeping all before them. The Irish selectors took the unusual step of arranging a trial match, but Tedford and his team mates would know that they were facing a challenge on a different scale to anything they had faced before. Basil Maclear had played in two nominally strong club select fifteens at Bedford and Blackheath early in the tour and had lost heavily on both occasions. By the end of the tour, in fact, Maclear had played against the All Blacks four times, and none of his four teams (the two English clubs, as well as Ireland and Munster) had managed to score a single point. By the time Gallaher's side trotted out at Lansdowne Road, the tourists had scored 646 points, and conceded only 22. There was, nevertheless, tremendous interest generated by the fixture, and it became the first ever all-ticket international rugby match.

The 15-0 victory was a fairly comfortable outing for the All Blacks, even though an injury had deprived the Donegal-born Gallaher of the chance to play against his home country. Tedford and his pack failed to stem the flow of All Black possession, and spent much of the game on the back foot. The star performer was 'Carbine' Wallace. After the tour he admitted that 'The best time I had personally on the whole tour was in Ireland.' He did not elaborate.

The experience had set the Irish selectors minds a-whirring, however, and they decided to approach things differently in the 1906 Home Nations Championship. Against England at Welford Road, Maclear was given the 'roving' role, but although he scored a try it was difficult to assess the success of the new formation. Tedford put in another outstanding performance in what was now a seven-man pack, but the relative weakness of the English meant that the jury was still out. As it happened, the powerful Scottish eight exposed the new tactic, and the Irish were well beaten 13-6.

The dominant Welsh travelled to Belfast for another Championship decider on 10 March 1906. A fit again Charlie Pritchard was looking forward to his showdown with Tedford, but the game became far more than an arm wrestle in amongst the forwards. The early signs were not good for the men in green, with half-back Purdon carried off with a serious leg injury. Tries by Thrift and Wallace put the Irish clear, however, as Tedford and his pack began to turn the screw. Despite Teddy Morgan's try cutting their lead, and a further injury

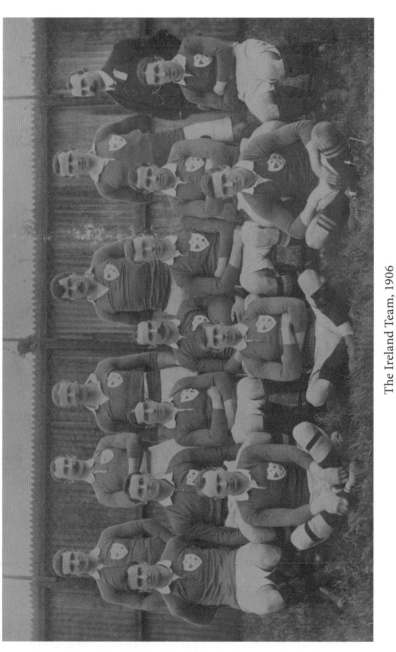

The Ireland Team, 1906

F Casement, HJ Knox, B Maclear, HG Wilson, M White, FM Hamilton (IRFU Pres),
JC Parke, FJ Gardiner, JJ Coffey, CE Allen (Capt), J Wallace, A Tedford, ED Caddell
G Henebry, H Thrift, WB Purdon.

to Tommy Cadell that left the Irish with only thirteen men on the pitch, Tedford stoked the fires of the Irish forwards to such an extent that it was the Welsh who cracked. Finally, Maclear broke free for a deciding score, and although the Welsh scored again, it was too late to change the course of the game. As with the game in 1904, the Irish had overcome the odds. Tedford's performance was key to what EHD Sewell called 'the greatest of all wins'. Charlie would have been keen to secure Tedford's shirt after that performance, however disappointed he would have felt to be on the losing side.

Tedford also played against the touring Springboks later in the year, and it turned out to be another great spectacle. The *Daily Mail*'s breathless report on the game gives an insight into the excitement of the crowd. 'The consensus of opinion about Saturday's match is that it was one of the greatest matches ever witnessed.' Maclear cemented his reputation as a big game player with a stunning try that began in his own twenty-five, when he scooped up the ball. Not pausing to think about kicking, he set off towards the Springbok line. His trademark steam hammer hand-off left the South African full-back on the seat of his pants, and he plunged over the try line. The *Daily Mail* was in raptures: 'No other player in Great Britain could have scored such a try'. Overall, however, the match was won by the astute Springbok players. One report noted that 'Krige won the match, while Loubser and Joubert were historic players. Maclear's try will never be forgotten.' When Stegmann's try clinched the Springbok victory after a stirring Irish second half fightback, Tedford and his team-mates must have been exhausted. For the Springboks, the excitement of the occasion was not confined to the pitch. Their vice-captain Paddy Carolin noted in a letter home that 'There were thousands of ladies present and the beautiful Irish eyes and heavy eye lashes were much admired by we poor South Africans.'

The 1907 campaign was another one that was marked by highs and lows for the Irish. On a personal level, Tedford would have been immensely proud to lead out the men in green as their captain for the match at Lansdowne Road, Dublin on 9 February. The victory over the English was wholly deserved, as two tries by Cadell and a try each for Thrift and the new skipper resulted in a 17-9 win. A defeat at the hands of the Scots, however, meant that the Irish were not confident going into another showdown with the Welsh. Tedford would have enjoyed locking horns with Charlie Pritchard – for the last time, as it transpired – but a 29-0 drubbing was a shock. A hat-trick for Johnny Williams and other tries for Percy Bush, 'Ponty' Jones and Rhys Gabe, all backed up by Bert Winfield's accurate boot, made the game safe by half-time. A fierce competitor like Tedford would have been infuriated by the Percy Bush try. 'His single-handed try was sheer impudence of one man beating the whole of the Irish backs', said one correspondent.

Sadly, the final defeat of the 1907 season was to prove to be Basil Maclear's swansong. He drifted away from the game, his military career drawing him away from the adoring crowds and focusing his attention on the parade ground. There were some who claimed that Maclear's body was creaking at the physical punishment it was receiving as constant focal point for Irish attacks, but he went on to take the role of Inspector of Physical Training at Sandhurst, proving himself to be (literally) fighting fit. He travelled to the Western Front in 1915, bumping into fellow rugby star Ronnie Poulton Palmer en route at Nieppe, where Maclear agreed to referee a match. By May 1915, he and his Dublin Fusiliers were trapped by the advancing Germans east of Ypres. His last desperate message to HQ read: 'Very many of our men are surrounded. We must have reinforcements.' None came, and Maclear was forced to lead a largely hopeless attack in an effort to break out of the trap. He was shot as he led his men forward, and his body was never recovered. Basil Maclear is one of more than 54,000 names on the Menin Gate Memorial to the Missing in Ypres.

1908 turned out to be Tedford's last season. He ended his international career at the Balmoral Showgrounds in Belfast – and again, the Welsh were pushing for the Triple Crown. There was no Charlie Pritchard in the opposition pack, and Tedford's team-mates seemed to be on top for long periods, roared on by a crowd of 15,000. Dickie Owen, Wales' veteran scrum-half, produced a Man of the Match performance in behind a struggling pack, living up to his nickname of 'The Bullet' as he fired out passes from the feet of the marauding Irish forwards. At the fag end of the game, Wales summoned up two moments of brilliance, and clever handling by Jones, Trew and Gabe supplied back to back tries for Gibbs and Williams. Owen was carried off the field on the shoulders of the Welsh forwards. The Irish had been robbed, and it would have been a frustrating way for Tedford to end his time in the green jersey.

A list of the post-war IRFU Presidents reads like the team sheets from Tedford's career – men such as George Hamlet, the holder of 30 international caps, Thrift, Coffey and, of course, Tedford, all played their part off the pitch. Tedford's time as President spanned the troubled years of 1919-1920, when Ireland was hovering on the brink of civil war. Somehow, the IRFU managed to walk through the minefield of Irish politics and emerge unscathed. Their players, in the words of the anthem, stood 'shoulder to shoulder'. This was no mean feat. The Easter Rising of 1916 had even claimed the life of Frederick Browning, the President of the IRFU from 1913. Despite the inevitable recriminations, and some furious debates over anthems, players from all the provinces continued to represent the island of Ireland on the rugby field. With the dreaded Black and Tans on the streets, and bullets being fired into the crowd at Croke Park, Tedford's time at the head of the IRFU can't have been without its pressures. Perhaps choosing to be led by such respected rugby men served to take some of the possible sting out of the debate. Rugby has tried to 'keep the politics out of sport' during the twentieth century, often without success. Tedford and his ex-team-mates managed to do just that, however, and this was as significant a victory as any achieved at Lansdowne Road.

The Pritchard Collection also features another Irish shirt. Emblazoned with the Red Hand of Ulster, it is an unmistakable link to Irish history and rugby. A tag on the shirt shows that it is a shirt that was worn at a match between Ulster and Leinster in 1912. The link to Charlie Pritchard takes us back to Newport, where a locum, Tommy Smyth, was based at the hospital in the town. He

was a popular figure at Rodney Parade. While Charlie was away with the Welsh team in his final home international season from January 1910, the *Football Express* was cooing over the Ulsterman's performances. 'Probably no forward in the Uskside pack has in the past four games shown more brilliance, especially in the open, than the Doctor.' Smyth played for the Black and Ambers on 36 occasions, scoring six tries, as well as winning 10 Irish caps. He captained his country against Wales in 1910, which was the game his Newport team-mate Charlie Pritchard withdrew from so that another Black and Amber, Ernie Jenkins, could gain his first cap. Smyth also scored the only try in a win against England in 1911. More famously, Dr. Smyth was also the skipper of the first ever fully representative British Lions touring party to South Africa in 1910, where he formed a potent break away unit with the star of the touring team, Cherry Pillman. Smyth's astute reading of the game gave Pillman licence to roam, and the Englishman did a great deal to redefine the modern role of the flank forward. Like Tedford, Smyth was a Malone man, and played for Ulster, and we have to assume that he was the source of Charlie's shirt.

SCOTLAND

'A day out of Hawick is a day wasted.'
Bill McLaren

'Scotland's attitude at the time was interesting …' said Cardiff's centre 'Rusty' Gabe when asked to reflect on the golden age. It was teasingly non-committal, but there was nothing neutral about his reaction to the 1904 England v Wales match at Welford Road. On a gloriously sunny day in Leicester, both sides played attractive rugby, ending in honours even in a 14-14 draw. The only cloud on the horizon was the controversy caused by the decisions made by referee Crawford Findlay. Having penalised scrum-half Dickie Owen so often in the first half that the Swansea man simply handed the ball to his English opponent and told him to try, Findlay then spotted something that all 30 players and most of the crowd had missed – a 'forward' pass to Dick Jones. In the dying moments of the game, Wales were denied a winning try. In attempting to put his emotions into words, the usually affable Gabe said that he 'always deprecated the tendency to blame referees' but felt that he was able to 'forgive and forget everything the referee did that day, but not the final decision.' In Welsh eyes, Crawford Findlay had form. Having perhaps had one more glass of malt than usual, he had asked Gabe at a dinner the previous year why the Welsh working class boys should be getting involved in the union game. Gabe recounted the fact that Findlay 'was surprised that Wales selected miners, steelworkers and policemen for their international teams and suggested that these players should join the Northern

Union.' It may well be that Findlay was guilty of pushing a point too far over Owen's feeding of the scrum, as the battle for the loose-head in the 1900s would have made modern scrum offences look pretty innocuous. The forward pass call on Dick Jones may well just have been a bad mistake. When taken together, however, there was a growing sense of 'us' and 'them' that Findlay's comments highlighted. What Findlay and others of his ilk failed to realise was that this attitude merely strengthened the determination of Welsh miners, steelworkers and policemen to prove themselves in the international arena. Bloodying the noses of those who they regard as the Establishment has kept the Welsh fires burning ever since.

The social mix of the Welsh side was, it has to be said, in contrast to the other home nations sides, and there were some dark mutterings in corridors about payments being made to some Welsh players. 'Professionalism' was a dirty word, and the RFU had insisted on sticking to the letter of the law over the so-called 'broken time payments' in the 1890s, even though it was bound to lead to the loss of a considerable pool of talent. The Scots, if anything, were even more Puritan in their beliefs, and frequently made a stand as the self-proclaimed keepers of the amateur flame.

The Scottish Football Union (later the SRU) refused to take part in the first ever British Isles tour of 1888 citing the creep of professionalism. Likewise, they refused to take part in the 1908 tour of New Zealand and Australia for same reason, and also turned down the chance to play the touring Wallabies in 1908. Their players travelled third class to games, and usually paid for their own tickets too. The home nations were put under tremendous strain by the league schism that opened up in the 1890s, but it is interesting that it was Scotland who stirred up trouble over a fund that was set up to buy a house for Newport and Wales skipper Arthur 'Monkey' Gould. What became known as The Gould Affair resulted in the Scots (initially supported by the Irish) refusing to play Wales in 1898 and 1899. The Scottish Football Union also had grave doubts about extending the Home Nations Championship to include France, as there were widespread reports of players accepting money to play. Later in the century the Scots refused to take part in wartime internationals on the basis of the fact that league players were involved.

On the field, the pre-war Scottish sides made a decent fist of challenging the Welsh in their so-called golden age. A look at the Scottish record between 1900 and 1911 tells an interesting story. The Scots were in a good vein of form too, winning the Championship in 1901, 1903, 1904 and 1907. Indeed, 1901, 1903 and 1907 were Triple Crown years for the Scots. They proved to be a consistently formidable proposition, particularly at home. Ronnie Poulton Palmer played for England on 17 occasions, and only lost three times. His England side was defeated by the powerful Springboks in 1913, and twice by the Scots. This is, in itself, an indication of the strength of Scottish rugby in the years before the war. Charlie Pritchard would have readily agreed – in three matches, his Welsh side had won twice and lost once, but the combined score of all three games was 18-12. In each game the Welsh forwards had to take the Scottish forwards on and subdue them before the backs could begin to weave their magic. All three games that Charlie played against the Scots were prolonged arm wrestling contests, where fire was invariably fought with fire.

The Scots were led by Mark Morrison, who was described by one of his South African opponents Jimmy Sinclair as 'a real rough house of a player and a great leader'. Morrison had made his debut against Wales in 1898 at the age of just eighteen. Within three years, he was leading his country, and in 15 games in charge he was only on the losing side four times. His fearless brand of leadership caught the eye of the selectors who were putting together a British Isles side to tour South Africa in 1903. Morrison, the arch competitor, has therefore gone down in history as the first losing Lions tour captain. As Sinclair's words show, however, he was not blamed for the defeat in the Test series, and in fact came home with his reputation enhanced.

Morrison formed a fearsome partnership with David Bedell-Sivright. Known in those distinctly non-PC days as 'Darkie' because of his dark complexion, Bedell-Sivright was also a player you would want on your side. As a heavyweight boxer of some renown he was an imposing character who positively relished the close order physicality of the game. He was widely respected and feared in roughly equal measure. EHD Sewell marked him out as a player who exuded a huge sense of commitment: 'He just played this game for all it and he were worth.' There were some who felt that he overstepped the mark on occasions. The *South Wales Argus'* much respected rugby writer 'Dromio' went as far as to say that 'he seemed to me to lack completely the chivalry which sets a crown on a great footballer'. For 'Dromio' these are strong words, and perhaps gives us an indication, a hundred years after his death, of how imposing – frightening, even – a figure Bedell-Sivright could be. Rugby is, and has always been, a game where players seek to physically overpower their opponents. It is a difficult line to draw, and intimidating characters such as Bedell-Sivright may have found themselves on the wrong side of that line on occasions. The Scottish authorities, so fastidious in their interpretation of the laws governing amateur status, were presumably comfortable with this fact.

Following strong performances in the 1903 British Isles tour under his playing partner Morrison, Bedell-Sivright was given the captaincy of the 1904 expedition Down Under. He was the only Scottish player in the party, but his ability to lead players of different countries was never in doubt. His team won every match they played in Australia, but the side lost its shape in the final matches after 'Darkie' broke his leg. Bedell-Sivright was a giant of the early twentieth century rugby scene. He died at Gallipoli, where he was serving as a medical officer, aged just thirty-four. The giant was laid low and eventually killed by an infected insect bite.

Morrison and Bedell-Sivright were the two dominant figures in a much-respected Scottish scrum. They perfected the art of the wheel, which allowed their back row to break off and dribble the ball at the heart of the opposition midfield. It was a tactic well known to their opponents, but these forward rushes were hard to stop. The selectors were sensible enough to play to these strengths and stuck to the traditional eight-man packs while their opponents (particularly the Welsh) experimented with seven-man packs plus a loose forward, along the lines of the All Black model. The seven forwards invariably struggled against the Scottish eights, and the advantages of having an extra back would be lost on forwards who were trying to contain David Bedell-Sivright. Crucially, in this period, Scotland were blessed with a good pool of talent to choose from. In 1901 the Scottish selectors played eight students against a strong Welsh side, and ended up winning 18-8.

Charlie first encountered the fiery Scots at Inverleith in 1905, which turned out to be Wales' first ever win at the ground. Willie Llewellyn scored twice, but was modest enough to attribute the win to a monumental team effort. 'Everyone played the game of his life' said the winger. One paper noted that 'There was a terrific fight between the packs and the pace was killing.' Charlie had experienced the dark arts of Morrison and Bedell-Sivright, and emerged smiling.

Seemingly unconcerned that they might be reinforcing a stereotype, the Scottish parsimony towards the visiting New Zealanders in 1905 backfired on them. The rugby purists at the SFU refused to countenance the All Black's request for £400 as an appearance fee to cover their travelling costs. A stand off resulted, and the SFU begrudgingly agreed to let the tourists have the gate receipts instead. Perhaps they assumed that the public would be unlikely to be too interested in a bunch of sightseeing Colonials playing a game of rugby, but the full house at Inverleith meant that they were forced to cough up £1,700. It is not known if the red faces at Scottish HQ were the result of embarrassment or anger. It would have been the latter when, after the tour, the accounts revealed that each of the tourists had been given three shillings a day as a subsistence payment. The whole Scottish leg of the trip was marked by a lack of hospitality – contrary to tradition, the touring side was not even invited to the post-match dinner. The row over payments rumbled on. A Calcutta Cup match with England was cancelled when the SFU discovered that the RFU had sanctioned the subsistence payments to Gallaher's men. Like elephants, the board members of the SFU had long memories and declined to play the touring New Zealanders in 1925.

Added to all this simmering ill feeling, in the match itself the Scots had the temerity to edge ahead of Gallaher's team, leading them 7-6 at the interval. An icy pitch and a hard-nosed Scottish pack made life difficult for the tourists until Bob Deans released winger George Smith into space very late in the game. George had been crowned the 100-yard sprint champion of New Zealand on five occasions, and his speed and swerve left the Scottish defence trailing in his wake. 'Carbine' Wallace remembered how his team-mates 'cheered him back into the field of play and shook his hand until it must have been nearly wrenched off!' Their sense of relief is obvious from his account. A few moments later Auckland's lock forward Bill Cunningham plunged over for a score that broke Scottish hearts. The tourists headed out of Scotland and began the rather more hospitable Irish leg of the tour. They knew they had been struck off the SRU Christmas card list – 'Carbine' wrote that 'We were about as popular as a plague of smallpox in the eyes of the Scottish Rugby Union.'

In the 1906 Home Nations Championship encounter Wales' new seven-man pack was demolished (perhaps predictably) by the power of the eight-man Scottish pack. Many observers were aghast that the Welsh should try this tactic against the likes of Morrison and Bedell-Sivright. The *Western Mail* glumly observed that 'It was hard to believe that this was the same Welsh pack that had played so well against New Zealand.'

When the newly minted Springboks arrived at Hampden Park in December 1906, they were 15 matches into their tour, but had conceded only three tries. They were as formidable as the All Black Originals, although it is perhaps the case that they have never been given credit for the scale of their achievements in 1906. 'Dromio' of the *Argus* felt that in his expert judgement 'The Springboks' conception of combination was better than the All Blacks, their passing was better.' It is also the case that Scotland's victory over Paul Roos' side has never received the kind of recognition regularly heaped on Wales for their victory at Cardiff in 1905. The Scots had only managed one win during their 1906 Home Nations Championship campaign and chose to blood four new caps – including two teenagers – against Roos' side. Surely, the rugby press thought, the impressive Springboks would run amok against this forward-orientated Scottish side?

The appalling weather in the run up to the match ensured that there would be no running amok, as the players would be ankle deep in Glasgow mud. It was a day made for the forwards. Springbok vice-captain Paddy Carolin wrote of the 'terrible condition' of the Hampden Park pitch. 'We scarcely enjoyed our first experience of trying to play football in mud up to our ankles with a ball as heavy as lead and as slippery as an eel.' One of the debutant teenagers, the outrageously gifted centre Ken MacLeod, caught a cross kick at full pace to score. The power and aggression of Bedell-Sivright and his pals then ensured that the Boks were pummelled to a muddy pulp. At one point the tourists had three players off the park with various injuries. As conscientious students of the game, the Springboks learned their lessons from the game. It would be nearly sixty years before a home nation beat the South Africans again.

On 2 February 1907 Charlie Pritchard played his last game against Scotland. Mindful of being overwhelmed in the past, the Welsh selectors sought to counteract the power of the Scottish scrum by picking the Abertillery powerhouse, big Jim Webb. It was all to no avail, as the Scots won 6-3 en route to a Triple Crown. There was more controversy during the game as a late try by Reg Gibbs was disallowed, another 'forward pass' decision that mystified the Inverleith crowd and all 30 players. One of Charlie's opponents that day was the Pontypridd-born centre Duncan MacGregor. Like his brother John, McGregor had started his rugby career back in Scotland, but retained strong links with Welsh rugby. Interestingly, he had played with Charlie at Rodney Parade in a match against Llanelli in January 1905. It may have been the case that he stayed in the town after playing for his old club Watsonians in the traditional Boxing Day fixture. After playing a part in the Triple Crown campaign, MacGregor spent the start of the 1907-08 season at

The Scottish Triple Crown winning side of 1907. Picture taken before their match vs Ireland, 23 February 1907. Pontypridd's Duncan McGregor is seated on the ground.
JC M'Callum, AL Purves, GA Sanderson, IC Geddes, DG Schulze, GM Frew
HG Monteith, ED Simson, WP Scott, P Munro (Capt), KG Macleod, DRB Sivright, LM Spiers
MW Walter, DG Macgregor.

Rodney Parade, appearing on 12 occasions in a Black and Amber shirt. After December of that year, he moved to his home town of Pontypridd, where he skippered the Sardis Road outfit. Despite their Triple Crown success, the Scottish selectors discarded him, perhaps because of their suspicion that his move to Sardis Road was financially motivated. Could it be that the Scotland shirt in the Pritchard Collection is MacGregor's?

The powerful Scots enjoyed a run of six Calcutta Cup successes before the Old Enemy moved to Twickenham. The move to the leafy suburbs of south-west London seemed to imbue the English with confidence, and it seemed to do what you would want your home ground to do – the crowd within operated as that elusive 16th Man. On their first game at the new stadium in the spring of 1911, the Scots were hot favourites to win the Calcutta Cup. On arrival, however, they failed to find the front entrance to the stadium and ended up tramping through the allotments to gain entry. To cap it all, the English ran out as unexpected 13-8 winners. The turning point of the match occurred when Scotland's centre George Cunningham broke free and headed towards the English line for what would have been a decisive score. A desperate English cover tackle resulted in a startled Cunningham still on his feet, but having had his shorts ripped clean off. He was so embarrassed by the sound of 25,000 Englishmen hooting with laughter that he stopped in his tracks, and the try was spurned.

The Pritchard Collection also includes a Watsonians shirt. The family is also in possession of a picture of both squads, taken before their match with Newport in November 1903. Despite the political difficulties created by the Gould Affair at the end of the century, Newport was keen to establish a Scottish fixture in their calendar. Gala had auditioned for the slot as far back as 1894, when they were beaten 21-3 on Boxing Day, but it was the Myreside outfit who became a permanent fixture on the seasonal Rodney Parade calendar for much of the twentieth century. It may be that the Pritchard Collection shirt was obtained through Duncan MacGregor, or perhaps swapped after Charlie's last game against

Watsonians shirt

the Scottish club on 27 December 1909, when a loose lineout ball was hacked on by Walter Martin for the decisive score. The single unconverted try sent the Myresiders home disappointed on that occasion, but the fixture was a popular one with fans and players alike. Watsonians were the dominant Scottish club during this pre-war period, and the match drew good crowds. In 1909, a young scrum-half called Eric Milroy made a real impact at the club, going on to win twelve caps for Scotland. 'Puss' Milroy died at Delville Wood on the Somme, less than a month before Charlie. He was one of 31 Scottish rugby internationals to die in the Great War. Milroy's mother was unable to accept his passing and convinced herself that he would return and left a light on in his bedroom every night to guide him down the garden path.

FRANCE

'Allons, enfants de la Patrie ...'

Monday, 2 January 1911 is a date that is highlighted in French rugby history. At the Stade Yves-du-Manoir, Colombes, the French recorded their first ever victory in the international arena, with a tense 16-15 victory over Scotland. For many who had worked so hard to establish the game in France, it was the day the doubters were proved wrong.

The omens were not good before kick-off, however. Fourteen members of the French team were scanning the crowd for familiar faces, as Charles Vareilles of Stade Français had failed to turn up. As Vareilles was in the process of emigrating to Vietnam to set up a plantation, his non-appearance at Colombes should not perhaps have been as big a shock as it was for the famously disorganised French selectors. They soon learned that their named substitute, Antoine Franquenelle, had missed his train at St Lazare. Suddenly, there was hope – Laffite, a Bordeaux player, was hauled out of the crowd. The other players started to piece together some items of kit for their new recruit. Just as Laffite was getting changed, the red faced Franquenelle turned up, having run all the way from the station.

These chaotic scenes were all forgotten after the French scored four tries to Scotland's three. Two tries for winger Pierre Failliot would have been a good warm up for the Olympic Games, where he took part in six different events. Inevitably, however, reading the entertaining account of the day is tempered by the thought of what was to come. One of Scotland's try-scorers was Cecil Abercrombie, who was to die at the naval battle at Jutland in 1916. Making his debut that day was Freddie Turner, who lies next to his great friend and international adversary, Percy Kendall, in the churchyard at Kemmel, near Ypres. Partnering the elusive Franquenelle in the French midfield on that famous day was Croix de Guerre recipient Marcel Burgun, who was to be shot down in his plane in September 1916. The knowledge of what was to come casts a pall over all the team pictures taken before the pre-war international matches. French and Scottish international rugby players account for more than 50 names in the World Rugby Memorial Book.

As well as taking lives, war also irreparably alters others. After hostilities ceased in 1918, rugby matches gradually returned to the sporting calendar. In what was billed as the 'Match of the Missing Eyes' two opposing props – Scotland's Jock Weymuss and France's Marcel Lubin-Lebrere – both had a glass eye. Jock was even reputed to have a spare which was painted up to look blood shot to match his real eye on days when he was suffering from a hangover.

Two years later, the 1911 victory was still France's only international win, and an (overly) expectant crowd of 20,000 packed into the Parc des Princes to see if the fledgling national side could repeat the trick over the Scots. As it was New Year's Day, there may have been a realistic chance that the Scottish forwards would be fending off the sort of Hogmanay hangover that makes a sweaty scrummage less than appealing. It was not to be, however. Festive celebrations had obviously been kept within bounds, and the strong Scottish pack gradually established a stranglehold on the game. The French side repeatedly infringed and the English referee 'Bim' Baxter repeatedly blew his whistle. The home crowd became increasingly restless as an energetic French performance subsided into a stream of penalties and missed tackles. At the final whistle, Scottish celebrations were cut short as an angry crowd spilled off the terraces and made for 'Bim' Baxter. Stones were thrown at the Scottish players as they followed the referee towards the safety of the dressing rooms. Drunk on the spirit of the barricades, the crowd moved off towards the city, where a minor riot ensued. Baxter escaped from the ground disguised as a policeman.

After a meeting of the Scottish rugby authorities, the 1914 fixture between the two sides was cancelled, and the two sides did not meet again until after the war. Relations between the two countries had been fraught from the moment the French arrived on the international scene. They had been criticised for playing fast and loose with the definition of amateurism, and the Scottish determination to defend those principles had brought them into conflict with the new boys of the Five Nations on occasions. Stade Bordelais had been indiscreet to say the least by advertising in the Scottish press for a fly-half. The 'good business situation' on offer to the kilted recruit would have had the High Priests of Amateurism choking on their night time malt.

Perhaps the 'Baxter Affair' was indicative of the growing wave of violent nationalism that was to engulf the continent in 1914, as well as an indicator of the fiercely independent spirit of the French game. Although the game had been imported from Britain, French rugby was quick to establish its own niche. France was the great exception to the general rule that rugby was the preserve of the United Kingdom and what Philip Dine calls the 'imperial bloc' – that is to say it's former colonies Down Under and in South Africa. The sport associated with the English and Scottish public schools was promoted by men such as the Baron Coubertin, the leading light in the Olympic movement, who saw it as an example of how a regime of discipline and physical exercise could breed a new, tougher citizen of France. The humiliating defeat handed out to the French nation by Bismarck's resurgent Prussia had led to an agonising period of soul searching. The soldiers of the Republic had been beaten in 1871 by their fitter, harder German adversaries, and sport was promoted as a means to put this right. Rugby was growing in stature at exactly this time – as the debris from the siege of Paris was being swept away, the very first rugby international was kicking off at Raeburn Place in Edinburgh.

Coubertin's influence over the development of the game in France was highlighted by the adoption of the Olympic rings on the first French jerseys. As an admirer of the educational philosophy of

Thomas Arnold, the headmaster of Rugby School, Coubertin was one of the prime movers behind the idea that the game had intrinsic value for French society after the defeat to the Prussians. As well as being credited with the modern Olympics, he was a rugby man, and refereed the very first French Championship final between Stade Français and Racing Club in 1892. He would have been delighted when his twin passions met at the 1900 Olympics, when France won a rugby Olympic gold. The home team defeated a Moseley Wanderers XV (the British representatives) and a German side. Hardly the pinnacle of international representative sport that the modern-day Olympics represents, but it was an important step on the ladder for French rugby. The shirt in the Pritchard Collection sports Coubertin's Olympic rings as it would have been swapped after Charlie's only game against the French in 1910. By 1912, the iconic fighting cockerel had been added to the design. The French team became known as 'Les Cocqs', which signalled the release of generations of bemused cockerels onto rugby pitches before international matches. Coubertin's rings disappeared altogether from the badge after 1922. The close identification between the British and rugby perhaps necessitated the birth of France's own creation myth. From the very beginning, there was an idea that the French played their own distinctive version of the same sport, a heady blend of artistry sprinkled with the occasional act of brutality. The French shirt was associated with a supposed Gallic indifference to structure, with indiscipline hand in hand with attacking flair. This stereotype is profoundly unfair to the huge range of talent produced by French clubs over a century or more, but their game needed to be distinctive enough to attract young athletes. The initial links with Britain were obvious – the first French club was established at the port of Le Havre in 1872, then sides drew on the sport's increasing popularity in the middle and upper-class schools in Paris, where the British Empire was perceived as a club that playing rugby allowed you to join. As Mike Rylance says in *The Forbidden Game*, his excellent study of the origins of French rugby league, union 'carried an exclusive label'. The first major development in the South West –

which was to be the eventual powerhouse of the French game – was at Bordeaux, with its ready links to the British wine trade.

Contact with touring British club sides did a great deal to help the spread of the rugbying gospel. The first recorded club tour resulted in a Rosslyn Park side thumping a Stade Français team in 1892, and although Oxford University's tourists enjoyed success in 1893 against Racing Metro, a Parisienne night out at the Moulin Rouge may have served to even the score for the hosts. A combined Stade/ Racing XV crossed the Channel to play in London in the same year. By the turn of the century, France had become a regular touring venue, and the lessons learned by French players and coaches were crucial to the development of their game. British 'missionaries' were tempted across the Channel to help speed up the development of the French game. The very first French side to play England featured Lancaster's WH Crichton at full-back. London Welsh's 'Boxer' Harding and Cardiff's Percy Bush enjoyed some time in France, as did the Penarth fly-half and coach Owen Roe. It was said of Roe that he 'came to learn French and never really did in 40 years'.

As the game gained in popularity, however, the French were able to find their own way. The sport's exclusivity was eroded by its widening participation and growing crowds, and eventually swept away. In the land of 'L'Ovaliste', the hotbed of the South West, rugby became the people's game, just as it did in the valleys of the South Walian coalfields. The game became an expression of the people's identity. Now, the Revolutionary zeal of the French crowd belting out La Marseillese has become as established a feature of international rugby as the ferocious Haka, or the sweeping melody of 'Hen Wlad fy Nhadau'. The French might also wish to point out that William Webb Ellis, Rugby's original rebel, was eventually buried at Menton, on the Mediterannean Riviera.

Eventually the four Nations allowed a fifth to join them in 1910, having played some 'friendlies' in preceding seasons. Initially, the fledgling French side struggled at international level, particularly against England. They first met at Parc des Princes on 22 March 1906, where a strong wind made passing and catching difficult. The

Red Rose forwards imposed themselves on the French scrummage, and two tries from Hudson put clear water between the sides. A French revival was snuffed out by a counter-attacking try by Raphael, and England had a lead of over twenty points by half-time. With the wind now in their favour, the French scored two tries, but the final score was a sobering 35–8. The revival in English fortunes coincided with the arrival of France on the Five Nations roster. The move to Twickenham seemed to make things worse for the French. In their first game at the Cabbage Patch, they endured another bad day at the office. After losing their full-back, fly-half and scrum-half to injuries they subsided to a 37-0 defeat. In these early years well-drilled English forwards tended to overrun their French opponents, leaving the field open for talented backs such as Ronnie Poulton Palmer to cause havoc. In the years leading up to the outbreak of the war, England outscored the French by 252 points to just 45, with 'RPP' scoring four tries in his last international against them at Colombes in April 1914. It would be thirteen long years before the French got the better of 'Les Rosbifs'.

France's first ever international rugby fixture was on 1 January 1906 against Dave Gallaher's All Blacks. They arrived in Paris on New Year's Eve having scored an eye watering 830 points against the best that British rugby had to offer. It was no surprise that the international debutants should be beaten by the comfortable margin of 38-8. The French took their job as hosts very seriously, refusing to allow a coin toss to decide who should kick-off. As an honoured guest, Gallaher was given a choice of ends, and the right to kick-off. The tourists rewarded such hospitality by scoring ten tries, but the French could take some comfort from the fact that they scored two themselves. Only an inspired Cardiff side had managed as many points against Gallaher's outfit during their ground-breaking tour of 1905-06, and even they had only managed one try. The Lyon forward Noel Cessieux was the scorer of the first ever French international try in what turned out to be his one and only international game. The French drew some favourable comments for their plucky performance, but it is interesting to note that when Gallaher and

Stead sat down shortly afterwards to compile their text book on the game, *The Complete Rugby Footballer*, they noted that 'individual brilliance is a beautiful thing to see, but it never wins a match of its own accord'. Were Gallaher and Stead thinking of the French match? It was 1954 before the individualistic France managed to beat the All Black machine.

Wales won all seven of their encounters with the French from the very first match in 1908 until the outbreak of the war, amassing 203 points to France's 39. The Welsh production line of 'Rhondda Forwards' proved to be too strong for the French packs. Allied to the wizardry of the Welsh backs, the French were bound to suffer, as they lacked the necessary cohesiveness and technical nous to challenge the all-round excellence of these pre-war Welsh sides. In that first international of 1908, the final score of 36-4 did not flatter the eventual winners of the Triple Crown. Charlie Pritchard missed the game as he was injured, his chronic knee trouble resulting in what became an enforced two-year international sabbatical.

Cardiff's Reggie Gibbs ran for the line for what would have been a record-breaking fifth individual try in an international but decided to turn in towards the posts to make the conversion kick easier. He was immediately tap tackled with the line at his mercy. He spilled the ball as he fell to the turf, no doubt accompanied by some choice Welsh phrases. Nevertheless, Wales still scored nine tries on the day. Charles Vareilles of Stade Français dropped a goal to give the French their first international points against Wales. Despite this hefty defeat, the *Evening Express*'s Walter Pearce described this lone French score as 'magnificent'. The memory of his only international score would have brought a smile to Vareilles' lips as he surveyed his plantation in Vietnam in later years.

The manner and margin of the Welsh victory in February of 1909 – 47-5 – would have been a sobering experience for the initially enthusiastic crowd at Colombes. Hat-tricks for Newport's Mel Baker and Swansea's Billy Trew were backed up by the dependable kicking of Jack Bancroft. The *Western Mail* was scathing in its assessment of the French: 'The Welsh could not help winning, the scoring of tries being as easy as shelling peas.' It is the kind of comment that coaches scan newspapers for so that they can stick it to dressing room walls to motivate their team. After all, sensible rugby pundits might reflect, only a single generation separated the Welsh from their own first faltering steps in international rugby.

Prior to New Year's Day of 1910 the French captain Gaston Lane said: 'I think Wales will win by 35 points.' It was an impressive piece of punditry, as Wales won 49-14. Bancroft, on his home ground at St Helen's, scored a record 19 points in the game, a performance not equalled until the Monmouth School wunderkid Keith Jarrett announced his arrival on the international scene in 1967. A last-ditch tackle by the French full-back Menrath had denied Charlie a second-half try on his return to the international scene, but there was a feeling that his fellow Welsh forwards had lost focus during a one-sided game.

The French centre Burgun correctly predicted that on this form England would beat Wales at Twickenham two weeks later. The respected rugby correspondent 'Forward' described the Welsh performance as 'loose and ragged', reflecting that:

'After a quarter of a century of strenuous and exciting contests with the three other nations of the Kingdom, in which the issue has been invariably an open one, it was too great a fact of the national sporting instinct of the public to expect them to place themselves to any inconvenience or expense to witness a game that was virtually won before it was played.'

'Forward' was perhaps summing up how many felt about the Five Nations new boys. During these pre-war years, victory over France was assumed, and the Triple Crown remained the big prize. Although a year later the 1911 Welsh side technically claimed the first Grand Slam it was only later in the century that the phrase was coined.

Charlie went on to play for Newport against Stade Français at the Parc des Princes on 8 February 1910 when the Black and Ambers won 15-3. Two tries apiece for half-backs Walter Martin and Fred Birt would have been an entertaining curtain raiser to a night at the Moulin Rouge. These two games, just five weeks apart, were

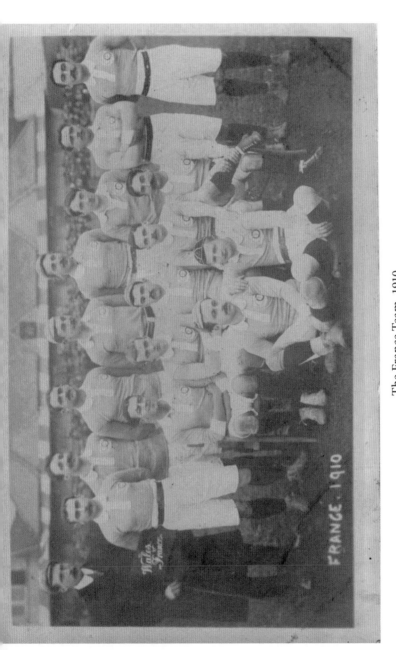

The France Team, 1910

R Menrath, G Lane, M Burgun, H Houblain, M Bruneau, C Martin
A Maysonnie, R Boudreau, J Anduran, M Thevenot, A Hourdebaight, P Mauriat, A Masse, R Laffitte, P Guillemin.
Six of the team died in the First World War.

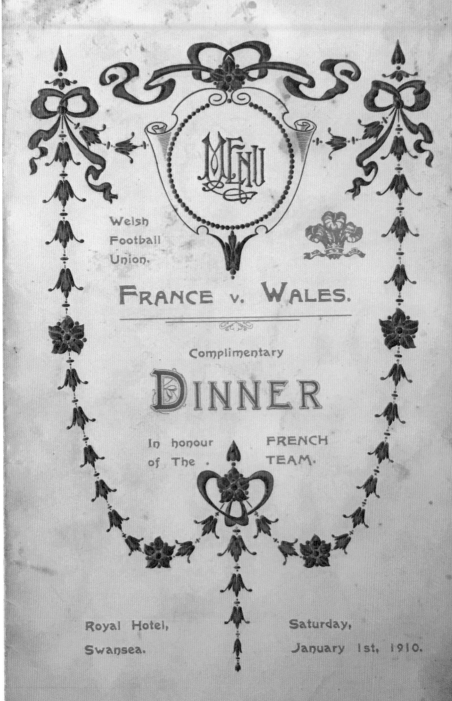

MENU

Welsh Football Union.

FRANCE v. WALES.

Complimentary

DINNER

In honour
of The .

FRENCH
TEAM.

Royal Hotel,
Swansea.

Saturday,
January 1st, 1910.

the extent of Charlie's experience of playing French sides. With his failing knee joint constantly reminding him that the final whistle would soon blow on his playing career, he would have been keen to swap shirts at the 1910 match at St Helen's. Perhaps he swapped with one of his more formidable opponents in the French pack – Racing Club's Pierre Guillemin. An architect by profession, he died a year before Charlie in June 1915 and they lie buried within a few kilometres of each other. Like his Welsh opponent on that day in 1910, Guillemin had been leading a trench raid.

In beating the Scots in January 1911, French rugby felt that it had made a point. The game had been imported, they acknowledged, with British traders and students establishing a rugbying toehold in Le Havre in the 1870s, and touring British sides helping to cultivate its growth. By 1914, however, the French side could claim to be more representative. Huw Richards points out that 11 of the players picked in 1906 for their Home Nations curtain call were Paris-based. By 1914, 19 of the 24 players capped in the season hailed from the South West. In 1906, world rugby took the French seriously enough to allow them to face the Originals – Dave Gallagher's widely feared All Black touring side. Although the New Zealanders won fairly comfortably, Gallagher wrote that 'in the course of time they will put a team in the field which will command the respect of any other.' Although the French national side lost 18 consecutive matches in the wake of that famous 1911 victory over the Scots, international opponents such as Charlie Pritchard saw what Gallagher had seen. Charlie would have felt the force of 'La Marseillaise' prior to the match at St Helen's, and understood that its grisly threat to make furrows run with blood could only be a sign of things to come. As Victor Hugo's Fantine says in *Les Misérables*, make a Frenchman sing it, and 'he will free the world'. French rugby would never lack conviction. Despite those early defeats, and the trauma of 1914-18, Charlie and the rugby world knew that it was only a matter of time before L'Équipe de France would take its rightful place at rugby's top table.

ANGLO-WELSH TOUR, 1908

'A cross between a medieval crusade and a prep school outing.'
Rugby writer John Hopkins, describing rugby tours.

The opening to the Anglo-Welsh tour of New Zealand and Australia in 1908 conformed to the letter of the laws laid down in *The Art of Coarse Rugby*, where Michael Green stated that the game should be 'played by fewer than fifteen-a-side, at least half of whom should be totally unfit.' When 'Boxer' Harding led his charges out onto the field at the opening game of the tour on New Zealand's North Island at Masterton on 23 May, they were almost consciously underprepared for the 26-match tour. In a direct contrast to the All Blacks of 1905, who had used the long sea voyage to gather a sense of a team ethos by talking tactics and practising handling moves on deck, Harding's men did nothing more strenuous than fight over deckchairs or for a place at the bar. Despite their studied lack of athletic engagement, the irony was that the Irish and Scottish rugby authorities had seen fit to turn down the chance to take part on the grounds that such tours were, in their view, encouraging the drift towards professionalism. In the century and a half of rugby union's existence, it would be difficult to find any project as amateur as the Anglo-Welsh Tour of 1908.

The dear departed writer of *The Art of Coarse Rugby* would be tickled to note that these pre-Lions were too wedded to the letter of the law to even accept the offer of substitutes during games, so played with 'fewer than fifteen-a-side' on more than one occasion. In the second match of the tour, the plainly unfit tourists would have been sensible to accept Fred Roberts' offer of a substitute when their full-back Jackett was injured. Their stoical – and to modern eyes, stupid – determination to play on regardless cost them the match.

The 19-13 defeat at Wellington was followed by a narrow defeat at Otago three days later, and the tour management team was already in firefighting mode. They would have told each other that they could hold their heads high, having played the game in its purest form, but the knowledgeable New Zealand rugby community was already writing off their chances. There was a growing sense of bemusement at the Anglo-Welsh side's approach, highlighted by their Pythonesque response to the blood-curdling 'Haka' at the start of matches. A shout of 'Rule Britannia' and 'Cymru am Byth' was followed by a rousing chant of 'Hip Hip Hooray'. The crowds were puzzled. Gnarled New Zealand forwards would have been licking their lips.

Back in Britain, the whole enterprise had received lukewarm support from the outset. The withdrawal of the High Priests of Amateurism in Scotland had been backed up by Ireland. The make-up of the rest of the party was sharply criticised in some quarters because it was not felt to be anything like a representative side, with less than half of the players having an international cap. Charlie's injury troubles – as well as his growing family and business commitments – meant that a place on the 1908 tour had been out of the question. The best of Welsh rugby stayed at home as selection showed a heavy bias towards the public schools. Indeed, of the 28 tourists in the party, 20 had been privately educated. The fact that Wales was represented by five old boys of Christ's Brecon did not go down well in the Valleys, the hotbed of the so-called 'Rhondda Forwards' who formed the foundations for the national side's success in the early years of the twentieth century.

One of the Welsh contingent in the 1908 party was RK ('Bob') Green, a tough and athletic forward in the highly successful Neath side. Green played in only four of the tour matches, none of them Tests. Although the party had a Newport representative, Roland Griffith, the faint 'RK' marked into the collar of the shirt in the

The British Rugby Football Team 1907-8
New Zealand & Australian Tour
Taken at Plymouth on Board U.S. Athenic

collection suggests that Pritchard and Green may have made some sort of swap. Both men were core forwards in the two opposing club sides, and it may well be that shirts were swapped after the epic encounter between the two sides at The Gnoll on 17 April 1910. The game was billed as an unofficial Welsh Championship decider, and Green's side came out as victors by four points to three. The veracity of the 'Championship decider' tag was hotly disputed by the Black and Ambers, however, as Neath's fixture list was perceived to be easier. Charlie and Bob Green may have organised a symbolic act such as a shirt swap to pour oil on troubled waters. Perhaps Green managed to get possession of a Welsh shirt at last – many observers had talked of his international potential, but sadly the Aberystwyth man was never picked to play for his country.

This fledgling Lions flagship for amateurism sailed on towards the rocks. The First Test loomed. Harding's squad had already picked up some injuries, probably as a direct result of their lack of preparedness, and their lack of a settled half-back combination was making it difficult to play with any sense of cohesion. This was despite the hands-on role of the team manager, George Harnett, who was described as a tough nut, supposedly well capable of controlling his charges. He sported a 'military grey moustache and a well-defined chin that would restrain any undue liberties being taken by anyone' but he was unable to get his men to march in step. The tour's anti-professional ideology meant that Harnett was powerless. 'The professional player ... when no longer useful to his club ... developed into a public house loafer,' he reflected. His own philosophy wedded him to the idea that professionalism was somehow inherently immoral, and strictly amateur players following the letter of the laws were the only bastion against the advancing hordes. Thus any pre-match preparation was somehow a betrayal of the way the game should be played. Harding's squad were, in a sense, held up as icons of the Empire. The Anglo-Welsh tour was an attempt to remind the Colonials of what rugby union was all about. It was a mission, a calculated counter attack on the growing appeal of league in Australia, and the creeping professionalism of the game at home and abroad. In a sense, it foreshadowed the rest of the twentieth century in this respect, with the more hard-nosed southern hemisphere Colonials establishing a clear advantage over the more traditionalist north.

At Dunedin they were faced by an All Black side that contained nine of the men who had faced Wales in Cardiff in December 1905. Frank Stead had already played the tourists at Invercargill and did not rate their chances. A two-shilling charge for entry to the ground had caused a minor riot, adding to the sense of a coming storm. Young fans were draped in the branches of trees to get a view, and a particularly aggressive knot of supporters outside the ground managed to tear down some perimeter fencing to gain access. The official attendance of 23,000 is bound to be an underestimate, therefore. They were rewarded with an exhilarating display of All Black rugby, as their forwards dominated possession, and the 'greats' from 1905 – Roberts, Stead, Hunter, Wallace – tore into the Anglo-Welsh defence. The thirty-two points they amassed could easily have been fifty, but for some indifferent goal kicking and the brave work of Jackett, who probably wished he'd given himself another couple of days to recuperate from the injury he had picked up in an earlier tour match. At times his reckless bravery at the feet of the onrushing Kiwi forwards drew some applause from the crowd, as did the tireless work of Leicester forward Fred Jackson. All in all, however, it was a train wreck of a display by 'Boxer' Harding's men.

The tour was now in a flat tailspin. At this moment of crisis, the authorities back home sent a short telegram to show their support: 'Jackson suspended. Return him forthwith.'

Jackson's name had been whispered in the corridors of power for all the wrong reasons. A stand out performance against the All Blacks was not going to save him. He stood accused of the ultimate crime – of playing rugby league, according to the RFU representative from Moseley RFC. Jackson had committed the sin that was to wreck rugby union careers throughout the twentieth century. One can only imagine the flap that this would have caused at HQ – their flagship project had been infiltrated by 'the enemy', the crusade corrupted from within. Jackson was given a tearful farewell by his team-mates, but he decided to jump ship at the first port on the way home. Soon, he was back in New Zealand. He married a local girl, and one of his sons, Everard Jackson, played for the All Blacks in the 1930s. The mystery over Jackson continued years later, and writer Tom Mather concluded that his name was actually Ivor Gabe, so Jackson was a relative of Welsh centre 'Rusty' Gabe. Presumably the name was switched to keep his league career under wraps.

For the purists, things went from bad to worse. Harding and the team management decided to deploy Cardiff's RA Gibbs as an extra half-back in the Second Test. This, of course, was known as the position played by New Zealand's Dave Gallaher on the 1905 tour, and it re-ignited the debate over the legality of the tactics. The powers-that-be had been quick to cry foul as Gallaher dominated the game around the fringes of the scrum. Now, the RFU's representative team had decided to compromise on its principles on this key position, which was in effect an illustration of how much pressure they were under. The decision to deploy Gibbs in the Gallaher role would not have been taken lightly, and their masters back in London would have been gnashing their teeth.

In the event, it proved to make a significant difference, as Gibbs' presence served to disrupt the flow of All Black possession at the Athletic Park, Wellington. The Anglo-Welsh side had produced some better performances in the run up to the Test, and the All Black selectors were perhaps complacent in awarding some new caps after the ease of their victory in the first encounter. More significantly, the conditions suited a 'roving forward' – in muddy conditions, there was little hope of any free-flowing handling moves. Harding's men hacked the ball on rather than risk a knock on in trying to pick it up, and their strength in the set piece kept them in the game. At half-time, the two sets of players were indistinguishable, resembling steaming creatures from the swamp. It was a nil-nil game at the interval.

An All Black scrum penalty in the second half edged the home team ahead. When it looked as though this could be the winning score, 'Ponty' Jones won a foot race as a dropped All Black pass was hacked on, and he slid in under the posts. In one of those moments that defined a career, Harding failed to kick the seemingly straightforward conversion to win the game. He was simply unable to get the heavy sodden ball up and over the cross bar, and the match slithered to a 3-3 draw.

Nevertheless, the Wellington mud tasted of redemption. The Australian paper *The Referee* described the tourists' performance in glowing terms. 'One of the best expositions of wet weather football ever seen in the Dominion,' it crowed. With some confidence restored, Harding's men beat Hawkes' Bay 25-3, where Bob Green made the first of four appearances on tour. Wingers Johnny Williams and Fred Chapman scored tries there and at Poverty Bay in a dominant 26-0 win. Maybe, the rugby public thought, these visitors could play the game after all? Perhaps this was the comeback?

Defeats at New Plymouth, Taranaki and Auckland brought Harding's men back to earth with a bump, however. In a moment that encapsulated the Anglo-Welsh's self-defeating attachment to the amateur principles, two of their men were helping an injured opponent from the field while their aptly-named opponent Ernest Dive touched down in the corner.

With the focus on the third and deciding Test of the series, the rugby press described how the All Blacks were 'being trained like racehorses'. In direct and rather painfully inevitable contrast, the touring team's hapless trainer TW Leslie was noting that his charges were 'sight-seeing themselves sick at Rotorua'. Rather than putting in some preparation time prior to the Test at Auckland, the group had decided to travel through the night to Rotorua to spend four days taking in the views. They were also gaining a reputation as party animals, but it is only fair to point out that they responded in a highly professional manner to the instruction that they should be 'home again before the milkman'. With Rotorua ticked off the list, they took the nine-hour train ride back to Auckland, with a couple of days to spare before the Test. Rain on the following day meant that they were restricted to a gentle gym session. Over-preparation was never going to be an issue for Harding and his boys. One wonders how they would have reacted to Wales prop Adam Jones' description of his days at training camp prior to his Lions experience. 'Bomb' summarised his days at camp thus: 'Wake up. Cryotherapy. Breakfast. Train. Cryotherapy. Lunch. Train. Cryotherapy. Dinner. Sleep.' Presumably the portholes in the cryotherapy chambers did give him some sightseeing time.

Predictably, Harding's tourists were routed 29-0, the biggest loss to be endured by a Lions side for the next seventy-five years. Even allowing for the fact that the Anglo-Welsh side were without star players such as Gibbs and Williams, and skipper Harding was injured early in the game, it was a final nail in the tour's coffin. The crowd celebrated nine All Black tries, including a hat-trick for Mitchinson. There was also a try for Bob Deans, the scorer of the famous non-try at Cardiff in December 1905. Tragically, Deans died just a few weeks later of complications as a result of appendicitis.

The touring squad would have been relieved to be leaving New Zealand, perhaps looking forward to what was on paper a gentler fixture list in Australia. They could be forgiven perhaps for heading to the boat in a more positive frame of mind. There was an enthusiastic crowd to wave them off. Amid the popping of corks on deck there was a cry and a splash. Bristol's Percy Down had spotted an old pal on the quayside, and had leant too far over the guard rail as they exchanged goodbyes. He plunged into the freezing waters below, and a few members of the party jumped in to save him. Down was eventually hauled out clinging onto a rope. Modern England fans will be heartened to hear that Manu Tuilagi was following in an established tradition when he brought the Red Rose Rugby World Cup campaign to a similarly damp conclusion in 2011. To add to the gloom for the management team, one of the squad's leading talents, Henry Vassall, had failed to even catch the boat. He was said to be 'visiting lady friends'.

The hard Australian pitches made life difficult for the increasingly weary touring party. Despite the supposedly inferior nature of the opposition, they were defeated by Western Districts and by New

South Wales. Again, the Anglo-Welsh failed to prepare for the Western Districts fixture, preferring to go out riding on the day before the match. The New South Wales match was described by the rugby correspondent of *The Referee* as 'one of the roughest games ever seen', and the tourists failed to convert a number of opportunities to score. A late penalty by full-back Kenna decided an increasingly fractious contest.

At this late stage of the tour, however, it was clear that the tour was fizzling out. By the time the tour had reached the union/league battleground, therefore, they had ceased to be able to draw a crowd. The rugby public had decided to vote with their feet, underwhelmed by the performances they had read about. This was disastrous for the RFU, clinging as they were to the hope that this touring side would re-establish union as the premier oval ball game in Australia. League's pre-eminence in Australia was hardly threatened. 'It is a wonder the visitors did not do very much better' said one correspondent, clearly puzzled by events. Perhaps he was guilty of not paying too much attention to the New Zealand leg of the tour. Harding and his players may have been guilty on that same charge.

In retrospect, it has to be said that the tour was doomed from the outset. In playing terms 'Boxer' Harding was the right man to captain the team. He had been outstanding in the 1904 British side, and was a widely respected player. Although born in Cambridgeshire, he had come to prominence in the School of Hard Knocks that was Welsh rugby at the turn of the twentieth century, and had been capped for his adopted country. It is clear, however, that his opposing skipper Billy Stead managed to get under his skin with some critical comments, when he portrayed the visitors as dour and lacking in creativity. The re-visiting of the Gallaher 'roving' forward role also put Harding in a difficult position. He was on record as saying that he regarded the tactic as tantamount to cheating, but had to swallow his pride and adopt these self-same tactics in the Test series.

When interviewed by RA Barr for his book *With the British Team in Maoriland*, Harding observed that in his view the New Zealand game was 'far too keen'. As a comment, it is highly revealing of an attitude that pervaded the game in the Northern Hemisphere for a number of years. It seems a strange observation to make, but gives an insight into the sense of aristocratic longeur that undermined the efforts of his team in 1908. The Olympian flame has always burned brightly in the union game, with its emphasis on 'not winning but taking part.' The All Blacks were drawn to the actual Olympic motto for their inspiration perhaps: 'Faster. Higher. Stronger'. Perhaps it was a defence mechanism for the British players, making it easier to effect a dismissive shrug of the shoulders when they were beaten rather than pound the walls of the dressing room in frustration. It is perhaps the case that the 1908 tour foreshadows the development of the game in the two hemispheres during the next century.

On the vexed question of team preparation, Harding was equally revealing: 'At home such a thing as getting a side to live together for a week prior to a match – no matter of what importance – is absolutely out of the question.' In a further blow for the sports scientists who think they may know what they're doing, 'Boxer' reveals the secret to his own athletic success: 'I indulge in walking as much as possible; it is a fine exercise. I am a smoker, but I knock off the weed for a week or so before an international match, and add to my walking a little running.' Meanwhile, it should be remembered, the All Blacks were 'being trained like racehorses'. The lingering suspicions over 'professionalism' – however that was defined – meant that no British side toured New Zealand for another twenty-two years.

NEWPORT

*'On the field he was a lion, off the field he was one of the
tenderest and sweetest of men.'*

Argus *rugby correspondent WJT Collins ('Dromio')*

The Newcastle-born Reverend Tom Graham was a major figure
in the growth of the game at Rodney Parade. He played for
Newport RFC between 1887 and 1895, and his florid signature in the
Minute Books from committee meetings held a decade later show
that he was still dedicated to the club long after he had hung up his
boots. During the course of eight years, he played for Newport on
185 occasions, only suffering defeat in a Black and Amber shirt in 25
games. Most famously, this tactically astute forward also captained
the side for four seasons, leading the Rodney Parade outfit during
their 'Invincible' season of 1891/92. His consistency and technical
ability were rewarded with 12 caps for his adopted homeland, and he
played in the very first Welsh Triple Crown side of 1893.

As a captain, he was instrumental in creating what was described
as a 'rugbying academy' at Rodney Parade. He was quick to learn
lessons in defeat, and would not allow his side to rest on their laurels
when they were winning. As well as refining skills, his approach
as coach and captain would be to substitute training sessions for
occasional walks around the town. It may be that this promoted
a sense of the club being part of the community, but for Graham
the appeal of these walks was that he could discuss tactics with his
players. In the off season, he would encourage regular midweek
meetings on Lighthouse Beach, where the players would play at

'knobbling', their own home-grown variant of boules with stones, play beach cricket, smoke and talk rugby. The Newport rugby archives, now held at the Gwent Archives in Ebbw Vale, contains countless receipts for match day and training expenses, including cigarettes. Over a century later, this last detail seems almost comical. As to the success of this 'Newport Way', however, one only needs to look at the results. Charlie Pritchard joined a tight knit dressing room of players who were well versed in the finer points of the game. Always a team man, Charlie's willingness to absorb the tactical and the theoretical meant that he was an ideal fit at Rodney Parade.

When Charlie came into the first team squad in 1901, he was captained by another Newport 'great', George Llewellyn Lloyd. Another noted tactician, he had played for Wales at the age of just nineteen, and led the Black and Ambers for four seasons. In 119 matches, he tasted defeat on just 11 occasions. There is a well-known sporting dictum – 'success breeds success'– and there can be no doubt that Charlie was extremely lucky to be part of a club with such a winning mentality. Nevertheless, this environment would have exerted its own pressures, as the standards were high. Charlie thrived under such expectations, however, and quickly established himself as a Rodney Parade favourite. The knowledgeable crowd was quick to take him to their hearts – the young forward never shirked a tackle, and was always in the thick of the action.

As he surveyed the Away Team dressing room in January 1902 the nineteen-year-old debutant Newport forward may have been mindful of the words of the recently departed Oscar Wilde. 'Rugby,' said the Irish writer, 'is a good occasion for keeping thirty bullies away from the centre of the city.' Charlie Pritchard would have been immensely proud – and a tad relieved – to have been wearing the same Black and Amber shirt as men like George Boots and Jehoida Hodges. These were the sort of players you dreaded playing against. Boots, at 28, was in his final couple of seasons as a Welsh international, but was destined to play club rugby into his late forties. Hodges would play on 23 occasions for Wales. These two gnarled veterans would chalk up over 600 appearances between

Charlie's club cap

them in the famous Black and Amber shirt of Newport RFC. They were, in the rather overused modern phrase, living legends.

Given a place in the starting XV by virtue of a late withdrawal, he would have been forgiven for feeling nervous. As Gwyn Prescott says in his excellent book *Call Them to Remembrance: The Welsh rugby internationals who died in the Great War*, the All Whites of Swansea were the top rated Welsh club side at the time. 'There wasn't a harder place than St. Helen's for a young and inexperienced forward to be introduced to the senior game,' says Prescott. Charlie

Pritchard would be only too aware of his place in the pecking order as he cast an eye over the backs as they prepared for the East vs West battle to come. Again, he would be comforted by the sight of his cousin Cliff Pritchard. A teak tough centre, the undertaker from Pontypool's strong defensive game had already caught the attention of the national selectors. He was destined to return to his home town club after five successful seasons at Rodney Parade, but it was as a Black and Amber that he was first capped in 1904. Cliff would have been a reassuring presence that afternoon. Charlie had always been close to his cousin and named his first son after him.

But young Charlie would have been forgiven for being slightly star struck by Cliff's centre partner that day. Gwyn Nicholls, the Crown Prince of a stellar Welsh midfield at the turn of the century, was to amass 23 Welsh caps, 10 as captain. He had been the only Welsh representative in a touring British Isles squad that had visited Australia in 1899. Nicholls is always associated with the blue and black shirt of Cardiff, but his work in his laundry business had taken him to Gwent in 1902, and he was enjoying some time with the Rodney Parade outfit. To an emerging young player like Charlie, it would have been a thrill to have been in the same dressing room as 'Prince Gwyn'.

The Newport wingers that day were Charlie Lewis and Johnny Williams, two greyhounds straining at the leash. Lewis had burst onto the scene that season, scoring 16 tries. He was unlucky not to gain an international call-up. Johnny Williams, on the other hand, went on to score 17 tries in as many games for Wales. Tragically, Charlie Pritchard was to share more than a Newport career with the two wingers. Lewis, Williams and Pritchard were all to die on the Western Front in 1916.

On that day, however, the debutant Pritchard put in his trademark tackles and scrapped for the possession that gave his cousin Cliff and Charlie Lewis a try apiece in a 3-6 victory against the All Whites of Swansea. East had conquered West, and a new Welsh rugby star was born. Less than two years later, in December 1903, Charlie would be playing in a full Welsh trial match at Tredegar.

Charlie played the rest of the 1901/02 season, gradually cementing his position in a pack that was beaten only once in the second half of that season, a narrow 6-4 win by arch rivals Cardiff. In the following season, Charlie was one of the first names on the team sheet, playing on 28 occasions.

Swansea were the only side to beat Newport that year, and Cardiff's furious rearguard action in February of 1903 resulted in a nil-nil draw, which deprived the Black and Ambers of the precious clean sweep over the Blue and Blacks. The Welsh captain, Gwyn Nicholls, was now back in Cardiff colours. The laundry business he had started up in Newport with fellow Cardiff back Bert Winfield had moved back to the capital. Now as an opponent a few months after Charlie's debut he would have noted the progress of the young tyro. It could not be long before the Welsh selectors would start to take a closer look too. Charlie had also scored his first Newport try early in that season against Moseley and he would go on to score twenty more in his career at Rodney Parade.

In the 1905/06 season, EW Gould was appointed to the captaincy, but the Minute Books of the Rugby Football Committee make it clear that Gould was not sure if he would accept the accolade, committed as he was to running in the forthcoming Olympics. 'Mr Gould asked that he might be allowed to consider his position', the minutes state. His reticence was well founded, for by December 1905 Charlie had taken over the captaincy. His leadership credentials were to be tested from the very beginning. As well as preparing for the Wales game on 23 December, Charlie's first few games in charge would bring him up against the All Blacks again a week later in their match against Newport at Rodney Parade, closely followed by hugely competitive games in front of big holiday season crowds against the Barbarians, Watsonians and Devonport Albion.

Towards the end of the 1905/06 season, Charlie played in a symbolically significant fixture. In April 1906 his mind may have been initially on the strength of the opposition – with good reason, as a combative Pontypool side inflicted a 6-0 defeat on the Black and Ambers. After the game, however, Charlie would be digesting

NEWPORT ATHLETIC CLUB
FIRST XV.
SEASON 1901-2

Played 28. Won 20. Drawn 5. Lost 3. Points For: 365. Points Against: 67.

G. THOMAS   J. WILLIAMS   J. ADAMS   H. G. THOMAS   G. SPILLANE   C. M. PRITCHARD   E. THOMAS   H. PACKER (Gen. Hon. Sec.)

A. G. BROWN   J. J. HODGES   G. BOOTS (Vice-Capt.)   G. LL. LLOYD (Captain)   E. G. NICHOLLS   C. C. PRITCHARD   R. CARPENTER

D. J. BOOTS   C. E. LEWIS   J. HILLMAN

the significance of the fact that he had just played alongside Wallace 'Chippy' Watts. It was that forward's last game for the Black and Ambers before moving to London, where he continued to play well into his forties. Watts was the last of Tom Graham's Invincibles, the unbeaten Newport side of the early 1890s, and the symbolism would not be lost on a student of the game such as Charlie. As it was, Charlie was in constant touch with TC Graham. As committed club men, they both attended the meetings of the Football Committee that was chaired by the ex-skipper. The Minute Books survive at the Gwent Archives, with Graham's copperplate handwriting detailing the everyday concerns of the club, from handling high level contact with the RFU to granting permission for Newport's Chrysanthemum Society to use the gymnasium. Graham's committee was even charged with the task of deciding how much to pay the club's pianist. Charlie's work on that committee marked him out as an heir to the Graham legacy, and he would have been proud – and a little sad – to have played alongside 'Chippy' Watts on that day.

One of the shirts in the Pritchard Collection was initially mistaken for a Barbarians shirt, but there is no record of Charlie playing for the Baa-Baas. The lack of the iconic logo on the front of the shirt had raised a suspicion that this was not what it seemed, and led to a closer examination. On turning the shirt inside out, it became clear that what we were looking at was in fact a time-bleached pale blue and black Cardiff shirt. An even closer look at the collar reveals the name of Rhys Gabe, written in faded blue ink.

Born in Llangennech in 1880, 'Rusty' Gabe had played his first senior game for Llanelli as a seventeen-year-old. He had the opportunity there of playing against the man who would be his international centre partner and mentor, Gwyn Nicholls. Soon, however, he left Wales for teaching college at Borough Road in London. It is sometimes noted that a feature of the South Walian economy in the twentieth century was the shift from coal to teachers as Wales' major export commodity. While he was in the capital city, it was inevitable that he should be drawn to the London Welsh club, where he starred alongside such figures as Willie Llewellyn.

The move to international rugby was not immediate, but it was inevitable. Gabe was quick and elusive. At over 12 stones, he was also a sizeable physical presence in any midfield. Injuries to others allowed him to make his Welsh debut in 1901 on the wing, and in his first game against England in 1902 he became newsworthy as the man who scored a try then promptly passed out. The legendary English full-back 'Octopus' Gamlin had failed to prevent Gabe from scoring but had succeeded in putting in one of his game-ending tackles.

By 1903 'Rusty' Gabe had taken up a teaching post in Cardiff and pulled on the famous blue and black jersey for the first time. In a sparkling club career, Gabe scored 51 tries, and captained the Arms Park outfit during the 1907/08 season. He was also chosen to play for the British Isles touring side that travelled Down Under in 1904, playing in all four Tests.

Gabe would have played against Charlie Pritchard's Newport side on several occasions. It is a rivalry as old as the sport itself in Wales, creating the heat of a derby match on each occasion. During the careers of Gabe and Pritchard the two clubs were, like the national side, at the very pinnacle of the game. As a point of comparison, Charlie played 219 matches for Newport, winning on 136 occasions and losing only 55 times. In the same period, he played against Cardiff on 34 occasions, winning only 11 games. They were often very tight matches – of the 34 encounters in which Charlie played 7 ended as draws, and 14 of the games were decided by just one score. They have never been games for the faint of heart. Even before the building of the M4, the rival players would have felt that this enemy was a little too close to their gates.

Charlie first experienced the raw passion of these games in February of 1902, when Cardiff scrapped their way to a 6-4 win at the Arms Park. A 10-0 Newport victory a month later at Rodney Parade exacted some degree of revenge on the city slickers. In the following season, Cardiff narrowly avoided the dreaded clean sweep against the Black and Ambers courtesy of a determined rearguard action at the Arms Park that ended scoreless. Charlie would have relished these dogfights, as forwards tend to do.

Two 3-3 draws set the tone for the 1903/04 season, but Cardiff's 21-0 dismantling of the Newport side in February 1905 was the only blot on what was destined to be an outstanding year for Charlie. With each season his influence was growing, and despite the fact that Cardiff won all four games in the 1905/06 calendar, Charlie scored tries in the first two games, and was always a point of resistance in a losing battle.

His importance to the team was underlined by his appointment as Newport's captain to succeed Wyatt Gould, and Charlie would have been only too aware that performances against Cardiff were by now an established yardstick with which to measure a Newport team's achievements. It is entirely typical of the man that he should score a try at the very end of the derby game in October 1905 that his side were losing by 17 points. Charlie had, in modern parlance, a 'good engine' and prided himself on playing the game right up to the final whistle.

In February 1907 an Alby Davies try brought an end to a run of six successive defeats to Cardiff stretching back to March 1905, and another 0-0 draw the following month meant that Charlie's team had stopped the rot. Charlie's leadership skills had been severely tested in the 1906/07 season, with the three weekends between the Cardiff matches being filled with fixtures against the touring Springboks, Blackheath and Swansea. This was all taking a toll on the Newport captain. His knee problems were becoming chronic, and he was only able to play the Blue and Blacks on three occasions over the next two seasons. When he returned to the fray at the fixture in September 1909, three Reg Plummer tries gave Charlie his own first taste of victory over Cardiff since March 1905. For the rest of that season, however, there was only a single cumulative point to separate the teams over the course of four hard-fought encounters.

In Charlie's farewell season honours were even between the two great clubs. A 9-8 Newport win in October 1910 featured a try by Billy Geen, a slight but elusive back who would enter Newport

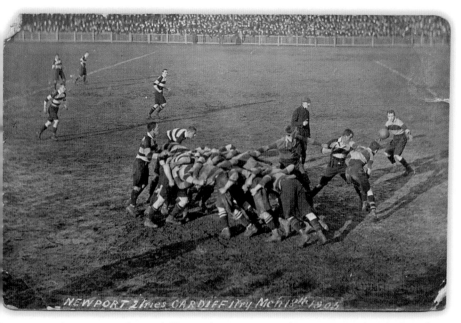

Newport at home to rivals Cardiff, March 18 1905. On this occasion, the Black and Ambers would emerge victorious, outscoring Cardiff by two tries to one.

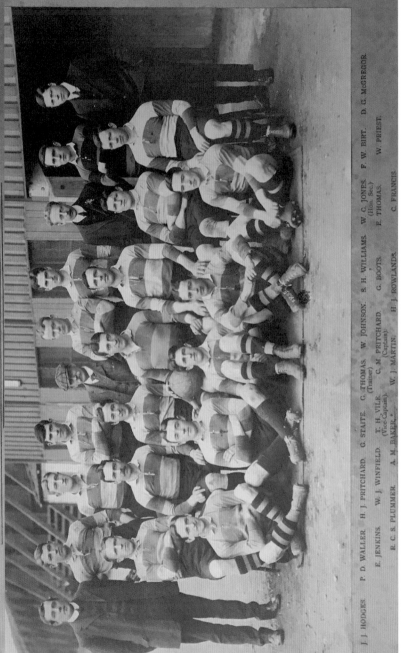

NEWPORT FIRST XV. 1907-8

J. J. HODGES. P. D. WALLER. H. J. PRITCHARD. G. STAITE. G. THOMAS. W. JOHNSON. S. H. WILLIAMS. W. G. JONES. F. W. BIRT. D. G. McGREGOR.

(Trainer)

E. JENKINS. W. J. WINFIELD. T. H. VILE. C. M. PRITCHARD. G. BOOTS. E. THOMAS. W. PRIEST.

(Vice-Captain) (Captain)

R. C. S. PLUMMER. A. M. BAKER. W. J. MARTIN. H. J. ROWLANDS. C. FRANCIS.

(Hon. Sec.)

RFC folklore with a try-saving tackle against the mighty touring Springboks of 1912. Tragically, like Charlie, Billy was also destined to be a name in Newport Athletic Club's Roll of Honour and is inscribed on the Menin Gate Memorial to the Missing outside Ypres. Two narrow Cardiff wins in November and February were followed by Charlie's last game against their bitter rivals. The presence of Rusty Gabe's shirt in the Pritchard Collection might suggest that his old international friend and occasional singing partner watched Charlie's last game against Cardiff. Tries by Walter Martin and George Hirst saw the Black and Ambers home by 15-10, and Gabe would have been only too aware that he was witnessing the end of an era. He had 'retired' back in 1908 but was still playing occasional games for the club. With Charlie's charity match and retirement rapidly approaching, the gift of the shirt may have helped soften the blow for his old team-mate. For Charlie, the win would have helped too.

On 17 April 1911 Charlie Pritchard played his last game for Newport at Rodney Parade. The opponents were Pontypool, and 18,000 fans crammed in to the ground to see what promised to be an exciting match. 'Ponty' (the nickname 'Pooler' was adopted many years later) were a skilful, physically imposing side, and the game lived up to its billing. In ideal conditions, both sides produced a full-blooded encounter, with Jack Jones leading the away side's forwards upfield with some strong carries. As Charlie and the Newport forwards began to exert their authority, Pontypool came under pressure, and a clever piece of footwork by fly-half Walter Martin set up an attack which resulted in a try by Newport centre Wilfred Onions. The conversion by Fred Birt gave Charlie's side a lead they were unlikely to give up without a fight, and they eventually ran out 5-3 winners. It had been an ideal way for Charlie to bring down the curtain on his Rodney Parade career – a close match against committed opposition, played right up to the final whistle. Just a week later, he was posing for a photograph along with his friends dressed in Frank Glasgow's All Black shirt.

He had been a Rodney Parade icon for ten years, captaining the side for three seasons with intelligence and bravery. He had picked up a serious knee injury in November 1908 at Kingsholm in a typically furious encounter against Gloucester. He limped back onto the field after some attention, clearly in some pain, but led the side to an 8-5 win. Modern physios would be shaking their heads – they would know that the chances were that Charlie was doing himself some serious damage. So it proved, as Charlie would not appear on a rugby pitch for five months, missing club and country games against the touring Wallabies, as well as the international matches in the spring. Irish hooker Keith Wood, when asked about his impending retirement in 2003, summed up the feeling thus: 'The heart is willing, the head is willing, but the body's had enough …' Charlie would have known exactly what he was talking about. Charlie's knee is heavily strapped in the picture taken before the charity match. His body had had enough.

After the international retirement of 'Prince' Gwyn Nicholls, the Welsh selectors had difficulty settling on a successor, and in the seasons following the famous victory over the All Blacks, Charlie was widely tipped to take on the role. Contemporaries such as Percy Bush would have been keen supporters of Charlie's appointment after he had proved to be such an effective leader at Rodney Parade. It is probably the case that the injuries that blighted the latter part of the Newport man's career also put paid to his chances of leading his country.

An article by Percy Bush on the man he dubbed the 'Uskside Apollo' gives us an insight as to how Charlie was perceived by his fellow players. Bush, as ever, made light of the knee injury that was to eventually bring Charlie's career to an end, but his affection for his club adversary shines through. In response to the gentle ribbing tone of this article, one wonders if Charlie might have countered by quoting Percy Bush's boss – the headmaster at the school in Cardiff where Bush taught. The exasperated Head wrote to the rugby authorities complaining about his assistant master.

'Mr Bush is constantly unable to attend school owing to illness or injuries …' It transpires from the letter that the headmaster did have some grounds for complaint, as Bush's attendance record was running at a pretty unimpressive 50%. This would be worrying enough in a problem pupil, let alone an assistant master. Some Welsh selectors would suggest that Bush had a 50% attendance rate at international matches too, and he was often at the sharp end of some critical reporting during his years in the Welsh team. One of the key issues was that it was felt that his style of play was not entirely suited to scrum-half Dickie Owen's style – and the Swansea man was very much regarded as the first name on the team sheet. As a result, Bush's international career is full of highs and lows – from an impudent performance against Ireland in 1907 that made the skipper for the day 'Rusty' Gabe laugh out loud, to a lacklustre error laden game against the Springboks in 1906. It was seemingly always feast or famine with Percy Bush, but he was a charismatic, popular team-mate.

It is interesting to note that in the article Bush clearly sees Charlie as a future Welsh captain. Cardiff's Johnny Williams got the job in the 1911 trip to Paris on the basis that he spoke some French, so by the end of the golden age there was no clear leader, and Charlie's departure had left a vacuum. Soon, however, the Welsh selectors would turn to a man of the cloth – the Reverend Alban Davies – to lead a ferocious bunch of forwards that became known as 'The Terrible Eight'. Famously, they fought – literally – their way to a win against the Irish in the 1912 Championship game that set new standards for on field thuggery. The players of both sides had even squared up against each other on the night before the match at a theatre. Charlie Pritchard had never taken a backward step on a rugby field, but a reading of his article on 'Vigour vs Foulness' (see Appendix) would be enough to convince anyone that this would not be his way of doing things. In the 'Uskside Apollo' article Percy Bush also describes an incident in a furious Cardiff versus Newport fixture when Charlie threw himself on top of a prostrate opponent to stop him getting kicked. Percy relates the story to illustrate how much his fellow players were missing him during his enforced absence from the game with a knee injury. Charlie was a tough, relentless player, but was clearly widely respected for upholding the values of the game.

Always a believer in fair play, Charlie believed in the idea that you should show respect to the opposition. The very act of swapping shirts is founded on that principle. Charlie had played himself to a standstill against some of the leading names in the game, and great players like Alfred Tedford and Frank Glasgow had exchanged shirts with him as a sign of that mutual respect that exists between rugby players. The game itself had gone through seismic changes during Charlie's short life. The RFU had been torn apart by the schism that resulted in the Northern League playing their own code, and the Welsh game, populated as it was by such a high percentage of working class men, was under constant threat. Despite that, Charlie would always defend the principles upon which the game was founded. The split with league would go on to dog Welsh rugby for the next century, but Charlie was a man of great loyalty, and as a leading figure of the game felt that he needed to set high standards of behaviour. The article on 'Vigour vs Foulness' was a viewpoint deeply held, and arguably as relevant today in its overall message as it was over a hundred years ago. Charlie Pritchard was one of the breed of men who made the game what it is and what makes it stand apart.

The Newport based rugby writer WJT Collins ('Dromio') had these words to say on Charlie's time as skipper of the Black and Ambers. The affection he felt towards Charlie is palpable.

'… As a captain he was not at the highest level, but he was a great forward and he was the most lovable man of all the Newport captains I have known. On the field he was a lion, off the field he was one of the tenderest and sweetest of men. There was a quality of gentleness in his manner, a note of affection in his voice, and great a player as he was, one thinks of him as a good comrade, a genial companion – a "very gallant gentleman" who laid down his life in the Great War.'

Charlie's last significant act on the international stage was to turn down the chance of a last hurrah at the Arms Park to play for

Wales against Scotland in February 1910. He knew that his time was up, and he essentially handed his cap to the named reserve, Newport's Ernie Jenkins. If he attended the match that day, Charlie might have felt that he had made a sensible decision. The field of play, said John Billot, was 'fit only for water polo', although Wales managed a pretty comprehensive 14-0 win. But if Charlie was hoping to further Ernie's union career, it was largely in vain. Over the summer of 1910 he accepted an offer to 'go north' to play for Rochdale Hornets, and by December 1910 he was trotting out on to the pitch at Coventry to play his first full league international against England. It is difficult to say if Charlie would have seen this as a betrayal. Ernie was a dockworker, and his exploits at Rodney Parade would pay no bills. A tragic accident in July 1909 had taken the lives of 39 of his colleagues on the docks at Newport when a dry dock wall collapsed and this event had in part fuelled a bitter dispute over working conditions in May 1910. With this sharp reminder of the danger and insecurity of his workplace it is perhaps no surprise that Ernie should be tempted to make the move. It is hard to imagine that Charlie, or any of the other men in the Newport dressing room, would not see the move for what it was – Ernie's chance to guarantee his family's future. Ernie trod the path that many working class Welsh union players chose to tread during the course of the twentieth century, and for the most part their friends and colleagues fully understood their motives. Charlie would have shaken Ernie's hand and wished him luck.

With the sun setting on his playing career, Charlie threw himself into the work of the committees at Rodney Parade. His own desire to see fair play was articulated by the Football Committee's concern over the club's ever-fractious relationship with their close rivals at Cardiff RFC. The minutes of 6 March 1911 determine the need 'to meet a deputation from the Cardiff Committee on Friday next to discuss the means of bringing about a better feeling between the players in the matches between our teams.' Perhaps it was in this context, with the charity match just days away, that Charlie was given Rhys Gabe's shirt.

George Boots, sat on Charlie's right in this team photo, described his captain as 'Charlie of the Lion Heart'

From the minutes of the same meeting, the chair Tommy Vile noted that 'It was resolved to grant the use of the ground to Mr CM Pritchard on 12 April for a match – Married vs Single – in aid of the restoration fund of St John's Church, Maindee.'

When he returned that night to the family home up the hill at Llwynderi Road, Charlie would have pulled out his precious box of shirts and started to plan the event. He set Frank Glasgow's All Black shirt to one side. That was for him.

1916

Yours faithfully,
Chs Pritchard.

THE DASH TO THE LINE

'My own definition of leadership is this: the capacity and the will to rally men and women to a common purpose and the character which inspires confidence.'

General Bernard Montgomery ('Monty')

The war diary of a World War 1 battalion was usually written by the commanding officer. In the case of the 12th South Wales Borderers, this literary task fell to the promisingly named Alexander Pope. A product of Winchester College, his brother had died in action in 1915, and his account of the movements and actions of the summer of 1916 are highly detailed, but shot through with the critical edge of a man under unceasing pressure. Pope was to go on to win the DSO in 1917, but tragically the terrible conditions that he so pointedly describes in the war diary were to result in a severe bronchial condition that ended his life prematurely in the spring of 1919. His ashes lie at his family's parish church in Stratton, Dorset.

Charlie's battalion was on the move at the end of May 1916, having completed their training at Blackdown. A photograph taken of him in uniform, dated 1916, is signed in his confident hand. His face shows the faintest suspicion of a smile, but his keen eyes and broad shoulders would command respect on the parade ground. Indeed, the six foot ex-international rugby player would cut an impressive figure in uniform, particularly as his charges in the 3rd Gwents were a 'Bantam' unit, so were all under five foot three inches tall. There would have been some excitement and not a little nervousness as they were herded onto trains taking them from

Frimley to Southampton. Then, in the early hours of 1 June 1916, the black mass of France appeared before them, punctuated by the lights of Le Havre. The 3rd Gwents were in the war at last and Charlie Pritchard had just ten weeks to live.

After an overnight stay under canvas at Sanvic camp, they were herded onto an excruciatingly slow train that took them eastwards, towards the front. Disembarking at Lillers, they trudged to their billets in Bourecq, a cheerless line of battered brick cottages on the main road to Aire. The South Walian boys would have seen some coal heaps in the distance, and wondered if their long journey to the front had in fact brought them back home. The gas helmet practice they had to undergo the following day would have brought any such day dreaming to a rude halt. The following morning, 9 June, they were led out of Bourecq on an eleven-mile route march through Lillers, Burbure, Ecquedecques and Lespresses. Pope notes in the diary that the pave roads were 'very trying to the feet', and no doubt the men took the opportunity to cool them off in the muddy stream that crossed the fields close to their camp.

The army's determination to educate the Gwent boys on the dangers of gas warfare suffered a setback on 12 June when a thunderstorm brought a lecture on the subject to an abrupt end. There was no time to reschedule, either, as they left Bourecq behind to move just in behind the lines at Houchin. Here, the rumble of the guns would have been growing, exciting some and terrifying others. Pope's commentary – 'We could very plainly hear the enemy' – gives us an insight into the concerns of officers like Charlie Pritchard. They would be fearful and excited too, in equal measure. Even a man who had faced down Dave Gallaher and his ferocious pack would have had to steel himself as he got closer to the danger zone. Leadership in the face of such fear was something that Charlie could understand. He would know that it would be vitally important that his team should see that he would not shirk his duty. It is, of course, the challenge faced by every military leader from time immemorial. You should not give your men the impression that you would not ask them to do anything that you would not do yourself. Whether he was in a half-time huddle in the rain at Rodney Parade, or issuing last minute instructions in a forward trench prior to a raid, Charlie Pritchard would always be able to lead his men from the front.

After a few deeply uncomfortable hours at their filthy billets at Houchin, the Gwents were moved into the Calonne sector of the front, having just been issued with their steel helmets. Over a hundred years later, it seems incredible that these trademark rounded helmets were not standard issue until 1916, and the British Army inevitably suffered many losses from the head wounds that would have been avoided with some effective headgear. Nonetheless, the new arrivals must have seen this as another indicator of how close they were to mortal danger.

And on the very next day, 15 June, Privates Edmonds and Day were killed by a trench mortar, and the Gwents would be learning that for all the bravery and discipline that a soldier might display, one day a random shell could 'have your name on it'. Perhaps even more than the idea of 'going over the top', it was these seemingly senseless deaths that did so much to undermine morale in the trenches. At least when you 'hopped the bags' and charged across No Man's Land, you were with your mates, and you had an objective. A random shell out of a clear blue sky offered no such justification. More Gwent boys were killed on 17 and 18 June before the men returned to Houchin. Although what Pope describes as a breakdown in water pumping arrangements resulted in only 'A' Company getting a bath, the (literally) lousy surroundings of Houchin at least gave Charlie's men an opportunity to come to terms with their first losses. Some of them might have attended the funeral of Edmonds and Day at the cemetery just outside Loos, where they still lie in the shadow of the slag heaps. A very final home from home.

On 21 June, Charlie and his men were back in the front lines at Calonne, having been served dinner at the abattoir in Bully Grenay en route. Given the circumstances, one would imagine that any ironic observations would have been stamped out pretty sharply. The trench mortars were busy, and the Gwents were too, rewiring some damaged sections of their front lines, and becoming aware of the growing threat posed by German snipers in the sector. One of their own snipers, Private Kemp, went down the steps into the officer's dugout. Shakily, he had to explain to Charlie and his fellow officers that he had shot and killed one of his own, a Private Oliver. He was buried at Bully Grenay churchyard under a bleak rain-filled sky. Another thunderstorm was on the way, flooding the dugouts on 23 June.

After another weary trudge back to muddy Houchin, the Gwents were given some bomb training behind the lines, and there was an inspection parade. Pope was clearly beginning to chafe under the burden of trying to lead his men in these appalling conditions. It was a common theme – staff officers a long way back from the front issuing pointless and unreasonable instructions. 'One suffers very much from indigestion of orders,' says Pope in the war diary. To add to the sense of strain, a young private in Charlie's company, Morris, had been sentenced by court martial to ten years penal servitude for shooting himself deliberately in the foot whilst on sentry duty. The initial sentence was a death penalty, but as was the case with 90% of such cases, there was some leniency shown to the young soldier. It would have resulted in hushed, subdued conversations at the billets and in the officers' dugout. Would the deterrent deter?

A few miles to the south, some of the most fateful orders of the war were being issued, and at dawn on 1 July 1916 the Battle of the Somme began. The British Army was about to suffer over 57,000 casualties in a few short hours. It was (and remains) the worst day in our history in military terms. Charlie and his men would have been aware of the action as thousands of massed guns attempted to obliterate the German trenches. The break in the weather would perhaps afford them a sight of an orange glow in the distance, and the damp breeze would bring snatches of the sounds of artillery pieces banging out their infernal tunes. Their own minds would have been on the tragic deaths of a couple of their comrades, however. Lieutenant Alfred Newman, the man described by Pope as 'almost unreplaceable' had been killed during a training exercise when a Newport boy called Wesson had dropped a grenade. Both men were buried in nearby Lapugnoy Cemetery, in a service attended by Charlie as well as other members of 'C' Company. A visitor to Lapugnoy today might note the inscription on Wesson's grave ('Gone but not forgotten. Mother') but hardly notice this small scale, almost domestic tragedy in the context of what was going on at the Somme. For the family from Magor Street in Newport, and Lieutenant Newman's in Small Heath, Birmingham, however, this was their own Somme.

On 3 July the Gwents transferred to billets at Barlin that were, if anything, worse than Houchin. Pope notes the complete lack of a latrine, and the fact that he and his men were 'waging an unequal war with countless bugs'. One can almost sense a degree of relief as they headed back to the front line near Loos, where they were given the task of repairing a 'badly knocked about' strongpoint called 'Doughty's Post'. Again, they would be attracting the attention of German snipers as they tried to manhandle devilish strands of barbed wire beyond the relative safety of their own parapet. A gas alarm at 2am on 9 July might even have had them dreaming of the foul billets they had left behind.

On 11 July, one of their machine gunners had a brush with mortality as a sniper bullet 'entered his helmet, ploughed a neat furrow through his scalp and went out again, merely stunning him …' The steel helmet he had been recently issued with just a few days previously had saved his life. The sense of danger would be only too real for Pope, whose brother had gone missing a year earlier just a few hundred yards to the north. Just over 50 miles to the south, the German defence of Mametz Wood on the Somme was etching itself indelibly on the consciousness of the Welsh.

The lack of progress on the Somme was beginning to exert its own pressures on Field Marshal Haig and his team.

Initial predictions for the July offensive had been found to be overly optimistic, and the next stage of the Somme was characterised by attacks that focused sharply on specific targets. Haig's 'Big Push' shifted from a war-winning campaign where his cavalry would be pursuing a retreating enemy across open country to a series of tooth-and-nail assaults on separate German defensive positions. As the summer of 1916 wore on, the talk was of weakening the German army. The language of attrition, of 'bite and hold', replaced that of a sweeping war-winning campaign.

In all this, it was crucial that the German army should not be able to reinforce its beleaguered defenders by stripping reserves from other, quieter parts of the Western Front. Raids and small-scale attacks were launched in other sectors to keep the enemy guessing. It is no coincidence, therefore, that Charlie Pritchard, along with three of his NCOs and twelve of his men should find themselves out in No Man's Land on the night of 21 July. He described the raid in a letter to his friend back home in Newport, Horace Twist.

'… so there we were, about halfway between Fritz and our own people, with the shells and other things hurtling overhead; but, thank goodness, exploding somewhere to our left. Funny sensation; you feel so frightfully funny and helpless. Well, there we had to lie. Luckily, the grass was long just where we were.

Fritz was putting up lights, and trying to make it as light as day. He evidently got the wind well up him.'

His letter to Horace Twist has the forced light-hearted tone of the officer staying calm under pressure. A rugby captain might adopt the very same tone on seeing a monstrous pack trot out of the opposition dressing room, and Charlie understood the importance of setting an example to his men in such circumstances. Back at training camp, the *Argus* had reported that Captain Pritchard had led 'certain hardy heroes' to take a plunge in the open-air baths. To Charlie, leading was an instinct. Just as instinctively, his men followed.

The night-time patrols were unwelcome additions to any unit's list of duties, to be sure, although it has to be said that the more aggressive types relished the opportunity to fight hand to hand. Faces would be blacked up, balaclavas donned, and raiders would be more likely to be wielding clubs than Lee Enfields. The purpose of these raids would be to establish a sense of control over No Man's Land, or, in the case of Charlie's sortie on 21 July, to locate and possibly 'neutralise' an enemy working party. On this occasion, a bright moon and some heavy enemy artillery fire had brought the excursion to an end. They had spent three hours out beyond their own trenches – a terrifying experience for all concerned, and another test of Charlie's ability to lead. A few hours later, they were taken out of the front line again. Their bad luck with billets continued as they attempted to make themselves comfortable in the bombed-out village of Le Brebis.

The first few days of August 1916 did not augur well. The Gwents were sent on more night-time patrols, returning with the news that the Germans had now cut the grass in front of their parapet – presumably not out of some demented sense of domestic pride, but as a means of clearing their field of fire. It would also make it more difficult to creep up close to the German parapet. The sense of the surreal continued on 4 August, the second anniversary of the outbreak of hostilities in 1914, when the Gwents were ordered to fire all available weapons in the direction of the enemy in a sustained display of hostility. The Germans were then treated to a rousing 'Three Cheers for His Majesty the King', and a rendition of 'Rule Britannia'. Stirring, if not entirely strategically valuable stuff. Sadly, on the following day, Charlie's popular commanding officer, Captain HC Rees, was killed by an aerial torpedo, just as he was exhorting his men to stay cool under the artillery barrage that had descended on them. He was buried at the British Military Cemetery in Loos.

The patrols continued. On 7 August, Captain VW Foreman led a small group out over the parapet and into the darkness beyond. They were tasked with trying to see what defensive duties the Germans were engaging in under the cover of night. With Foreman was a Lieutenant Harrison, whose first raid this was going to be, a trusted NCO in the shape of Sergeant Walters, and two Privates, Jones and Banwell. As suspected, they found the German fatigue group hard at work. Foreman decided that they needed to get closer, so started to attempt to cut a path through the German wire. In doing so, they were spotted, and the alarm was raised. The war diary states that an unnamed member of the party then attempted to throw a grenade, but it fell short, mortally wounding Private Banwell. Foreman was also wounded, but was carried back by Private Jones. Despite his own injuries, Jones then returned into No Man's Land to help Harrison. These selfless actions earned the young private a Military Medal. Despite further searches, the body of Private Banwell was never found, and he is named on the Loos Memorial to the Missing. All of this underlined the dangers inherent in these raids. Both sides were very much aware of movements in the strip of land that separated their respective lines, and were ready to react with maximum force to any incursions. The artillery on both sides stood ready to pepper these zones, and machine guns were carefully positioned to create 'killing zones'. Even though defenders would be firing blind at night, raiding parties knew that the curtain of fire that would descend on them should they be rumbled would be deadly.

Nevertheless, the war diary describes another 'special patrol' that crawls out into the night on 12 August. This time it was led by Captain Pritchard. His team were looking for likely gaps in the German wire in preparation for another, bigger raid. The Germans were observed at work again, fixing sections of wire. It was noted that three sentries were set to patrol those gaps. On the following night, Sunday, 13 August, this intelligence was to be put to use. Charlie was to lead a full-scale raid from a position called 'T Head Sap'. The aim – to attack the enemy position, and attempt to bring a German soldier back to the British trenches to be interrogated.

Pope's account of the affair begins in triumphalist mode, 'The Battalion is congratulating itself today upon the accomplishment of a quite successful raid on an enemy trench last night …' The raiding party had in fact reached the enemy line and had inflicted casualties. A German soldier had indeed been captured. The loss of one man, Private Masden, is noted, as is the fact that a Private Pickett would be among a group of five men who would be recommended for a medal. There is also a reference to the fact that Captain CM Pritchard had been wounded.

A preliminary bombardment had allowed Pritchard's party to rush the opposing trenches. Charlie was shot through the wrist as he dropped into the German trench, but refused aid, knowing that what had to be done had to be done quickly. The wound did not stop him subduing a Bavarian soldier with his bare hands, then he bundled him up over the parapet. As he led his men back across No Man's Land, the German defence began to bite back, and Charlie was hit again. It is not certain if this was a shrapnel or a bullet wound, but Charlie had been hit at the top of the thigh, and he was bleeding heavily. He handed the prisoner over to one of his junior officers. Now on the edge of consciousness, Charlie was helped back to the British line by Lieutenant Enright and Private Pickett and put on a stretcher. The bantam Gwent stretcher-bearers must have struggled to bear the weight of the now unconscious ex-rugby international down the narrow slippery communication trenches. By this time, Pope notes that German artillery and machine guns were opening up all over the sector.

Pope's tone changes on the following day, when news of Charlie's death at the Casualty Clearing Station at Chocques filters through.

'This morning we heard to our great sorrow that Captain CM Pritchard had died of his wounds. The Battalion thus loses a very gallant officer and a chivalrous, generous, and large-minded gentleman.'

A letter home by Company Sergeant Major Codling gives an account of the action, and reflects the shock felt by the Gwents at the loss of such a widely respected officer.

'Well, old boy, we are not so cheerful at present, for no doubt you have heard of the very severe blow this battalion has had in losing our dear old friend, Captain Pritchard. He was undoubtedly the best we had, or ever will have. It happened on Saturday night last. Our battalion made a bombing raid on the German trenches, led by Captain Pritchard, Lieutenant Enright (friend of our chief) and another officer. The raid was a great success, but in my opinion all the raids in this war were never worth the life of such a man as Captain Pritchard. During the time the raid was on our guns played havoc all along the lines – it was a sight, I can tell you, one mass of smoke and flame; at the same time our boys were putting bombs into their trenches. It's a marvel how our boys got back as they did. I happened to go along the line and was near when Captain Pritchard was brought in, so assisted to get him into a dugout to be attended to.

However we got him in I don't know, for he was such a weight. I can tell you he stuck it well, quite sensible. He asked the doctor if he had any chance. "Tell me," he said. And the doctor told him "Yes." He was in an awful mess, and I cut his breeches from him; then you could see the wound in his right buttock, his left wrist (I believe it was) and breast. They had brought a prisoner in, you know, and he asked "Have they got the Hun?" And they said "Yes, Pritch, he is in all right." Then he said, "Well, I have done my bit." And he had, poor chap; for the news came through yesterday morning that he had died of his wounds. I can assure you it was a terrible shock to us for he was loved by all. We did think he would pull through, but we are told it was through losing so much blood.'

Back at 5, Llwynderi Road, Newport, the pregnant and newly-widowed Florence received a letter from Lt. Col. Alexander expressing his sorrow at the loss of Charlie. He wrote that her husband was recommended for a Military Cross, noting that 'Had he lived he would without doubt have received the decoration.' No doubt meant well, but one senses that his words would have rung hollow. She was due to give birth at the end of the year, and would have worried about their young sons Cliff (12) and Mick (6). Like so many women widowed by the war, there would be daily reminders of their loss. In December of 1916, Violet was born, the daughter Charlie never met. Throughout her life, she had to contend with awkward conversations with people who knew and admired her father, a man she never knew. On 14 August each year, her mother

CAPTAIN C. M. PRITCHARD.

"Loved by All."

How He was Brought In.

Following extract from a letter, written to a member of the Newport Borough Police by Company Sergeant-Major Codling, dated Tuesday, August 15, will be read with emotion by Captain Charlie Pritchard's friends:—

"Well, old boy, we are not so cheerful at present, for no doubt you have heard of the very severe blow this battalion has had in losing our dear old friend, Captain Pritchard. He was undoubtedly the best we had, or ever will have. It happened on Saturday night last. Our battalion made a bombing raid on the German trenches, led by Captain Pritchard, Lieutenant Enright (friend of our chief), and another officer. The raid was a great success, but in my opinion all the raids in this war were never worth the life of such a man as Captain Pritchard. During the time the raid was on our guns played havoc all along their lines—it was a sight, I can tell you, one mass of smoke and flame; at the same time our boys were there putting bombs into their trenches. It's a marvel how our boys got back as they did. I happened to go along the line, and was near when Captain Pritchard was brought in, so assisted to get him into a dug-out to be attended to. However, we got him in I don't know, for he was such a weight. I can tell you he stuck it well, quite sensible. He asked the doctor if he had any chance. 'Tell me,' he said. And the doctor told him, 'Yes.' He was in an awful mess, and I cut his breeches from him; then we could see he had the wound in his right buttock, his left wrist (I believe it was), and breast. They brought a prisoner in, you know, and he asked, 'Have they got the Hun?' And they said 'Yes, Pritch., he is, in all right.' Then he said, 'Well, I have done my bit.' And he had, poor chap; for the news came through yesterday morning that he had died of his wounds. I can assure you it was a terrible shock to us, for he was loved by all. We did think he would pull through, but we are told it was through losing so much blood. I can't say what he was hit with—may have been shrapnel, or a bomb."

would go out into the garden and cut one of the roses from one of the bushes so carefully propagated by her late husband. After she placed it in a vase on the kitchen table Florence would go to bed, unable to face the pain of that day. Violet grew up with the date of her father's death being a black day in the Pritchard household. It is perhaps no surprise that she too died on 14 August 1985.

The Memorial Gates at Rodney Parade

APPENDIX

An article from a contemporary magazine called *Jones Rugby* (date uncertain)

VIGOUR v. FOULNESS by CM Pritchard (Newport and Wales)
Rugby Football is a vigorous game. That is part of its attraction. It is not a game for weaklings. That is why it delights the British race, who glory in strength. It is a game for men who are physically sound, for men who are ready and able to take some hard knocks, for no matter how cleanly and scientifically it may be played there is always the chance of a pretty severe shaking in a hard tackle, or an accidental kick in the loose. It is a game in which strength and weight are valuable qualities – not the most valuable, of course: it is a game in which a player is justified in using weight and strength; and no one would seek to deny that many a famous rugby player has 'delighted as a giant to run his course' – leaving strewn by the way men who went down before an effective 'hand off' when they tried to stay his course by 'going high'.

Yes, Rugby Football is essentially a vigorous game, and it would lose half its charm as a game and as a spectacle if it were played in a namby-pampy spirit; but there is always the danger that there may creep into the game vigour which reaches or passes the verge of brutality – that it may be degraded by foulness; and the object of this article is to uphold legitimate vigour and to condemn foul play in all its forms.

WHAT IS LEGITIMATE VIGOUR?
It is necessary to differentiate between legitimate vigour and unfair roughness, and to outsiders there is often difficulty in doing this. The spectator sees the man with the ball go down, with a 13 stone or 14 stone tackler on top of him. If the man with the ball goes down awkwardly, he may get up with a broken collar bone or dented ribs. These injuries may be the result of legitimate vigour, or they may be due to unfair roughness. There is probably only one man who knows – the tackler. He

is probably quite conscious whether his intention was simply to tackle his man, or whether in his mind there was the desire not only to stop his progress and to prevent him passing but to 'take as much out of him as possible' by coming down heavily on top of him. If there is any desire to hurt an opponent – not to go so far as breaking his ribs or his collar bone, of course, but to render him less able to play by injuring him in any way – the tackler has been guilty of unfair roughness. Motive counts in football as in the law courts. To attempt to hurt an opponent is foreign to the spirit and the law of the game, and the man who uses vigour with the desire and intention to injure an opponent is no sportsman. A man is perfectly justified in going hard for a man he wishes to tackle – whether he goes high or low (and if he is wise he will go low) he has a right to put him down so that there is no mistake about it; but where a big heavy forward is tackling a 9 stone half-back or a slim young wing three-quarter he is not called upon to bump the little fellow on the ground and fall upon him as heavily as possible. If he can only tackle him by going down on him, he is bound to do it, but wanton roughness, or anything that in the nature of heavy charging of lightweights by heavy men, is outside the limits of legitimate vigour. Thank goodness, there is room for chivalry in the game, and lots of big strong men who delight in putting out all their strength when they have to deal with men of their own weight, know how to restrain themselves when they meet players three or four stone lighter than them. Let a man charge or tackle vigorously, but there should be no desire or attempt to hurt an opponent; and if a man who is running with the ball has an opportunity to 'hand off' an opponent let him do it with the intention of sending him spinning; but there must be no clenched fist, no open fingers jabbed in a man's face to the danger of his eyes. It must be a clean 'hand off', not only with no desire to hurt an opponent, but with care not to injure or endanger him.

TRICKY FOULS
Foulness in football may be divided into two kinds – tricky foulness and brutal foulness. There are technical 'fouls' – breaches of the law which are penalised if detected, which do not call for the same

condemnation as the mean, dirty, and dangerous tricks which sometimes are played by men determined to win at any price, or the wilful brutality and culpable recklessness which seeks an advantage at the cost of injury to an opponent. To deal with tricky fouling first, one may point to the tripping which is often practised to prevent a man from continuing a dribble or to stop a man who is running when he cannot be tackled. Some players are very clever in this direction, and some display their cleverness by playing their tricks when the referee cannot (or is not likely to) see them. Some of these practiced foulers are perfectly well aware that the referee's eyes are on the ball, and they trip up not the man who is dribbling or carrying the ball, but the man who is following up in a position to continue the effect. There are men who are very clever at holding an opponent in order to prevent him from following up – it is wonderful how smartly some of them conceal their action from the referee, especially when a body of men are following up together, though their tricks are visible to a section of the spectators.

Another foul which is becoming extremely common, and ought to be dealt with very stringently by referees, is the practice of pushing at the line out. A man is waiting for the ball at the throw out from touch, he sees that it is coming to him, but while his eyes are on the ball, perhaps as he is jumping for it, he is vigorously pushed by an opponent, so that he may not catch. It is an absolute foul – entirely against the spirit of the game. Sometimes when there is a doubt as to where the ball is coming, two or three men will be pushed, so that none of them may get the ball. In some teams it sometimes seems as if there were a definite understanding between two players that one should push an opponent and that the other should take the ball – combination in foulness.

Another form of tricky foulness which is sometimes practiced is that when an attack is in progress one of the attacking side will deliberately cut across between the man with the ball and a tackler who is trying to get at him. I remember a case in which this enabled the offending side to score, since the man who played the obstructing game so effectively checked a fast opponent who could have tackled the man with the ball that he simply could not get near him. There are cases where the players deliberately tackle opponents who have not the ball in order that he may not follow up to take a pass; and it is far too common a trick to tackle a man who has given a pass in order that he may not follow up to take a re-pass. This is especially the case, of course, where a clever bit of inter-passing has been started and a score seems possible. Two men – perhaps the two halves, perhaps the inside half and the wing three-quarter – have got away on the blind side of the scrummage and the inside half, having given a pass, has received the ball again. The half or wing who has given the ball has beaten the opposing wing by the pass, and as he is not in possession of the ball there is no justification for any opponent to touch him. He intends to follow up, he means to be in position to take another pass when his fellow player faces the full-back. But no! The opposing wing three-quarter sees the danger ahead, and to prevent it he tackles a man who has not the ball and puts him down. There are cases where the interval between the pass and the tackle is so slight that there may be some justification for the plea that it was impossible to pull up; but there are far more cases where the tackle is deliberate foul play. The man who is attacked is not injured, but he has been robbed of a scoring chance by a tricky foul.

There are fouls of both kinds in and around the scrum. To hand the ball out is an audacious foul, but there are men who will risk it – just as they will risk any penalty if they think it will pay them. There are men, too, who deliberately trip the opposing inside half as he comes round the scrum to attempt a tackle, while it is wonderful how many men are put down without the ball in a strenuous game.

BRUTAL FOULNESS
When a man not only breaks the law but also injures an opponent, that is brutal foulness. A trip may be either a tricky or a brutal foul. If a man is 'hacked' over, it is almost invariably brutal, for it cannot be done without causing pain. It is unfortunately borne in upon one that there are players who deliberately try to injure their opponents. I do not say that they wish to hurt them seriously or permanently, but they are willing to give a man a kick, or to charge him roughly enough to

lay him out. Often you hear an inside half say : 'As I was going round the scrum, he kicked me clean off my feet.' That means that one of the opposing forwards, after his side had heeled the ball, shot out his leg and hacked the half-back over.

Another form of brutal foulness is wild, reckless, or wilful kicking when a man has gone down to the ball. There are men who seem to think that they have a right to kick a man off the ball if he falls upon it to check a rush, and there is far too much kicking on such occasions. (see Note 1 at end)

Another common form of brutality is the heavy charging of a man after he has got in his kick. Again it may be argued that this may be accidental. So it may be in some cases, for a really fast forward may be unable to stop himself; but there are very many instances where a man has got in his kick and there is quite a considerable interval before the opposing player dashes into him and charges him over. (Note 2) In some cases men not only make no effort to check themselves in order to avoid impact, but deliberately charge into a full-back as hard as they can. Worse than that, there are players who charge with a view to doing as much damage as possible – who put their heads down as if they were attempting to tackle, and charge with their shoulders into the short ribs of the fullback who is half turned to catch the ball, or of a forward who is jumping for the ball at the line-out. It is hardly necessary to say that attempts to throw or charge an opponent into the rails, to charge him unexpectedly when he is over the touch-line, to use the clenched fist under any circumstances, to 'scrag' – half-strangle a man by tackling him round the throat, or to kick or strike a man in the scrum is foul play.

'PLAY THE GAME'

It is unfortunately true that there is in football today (and let it not be supposed that I refer only to Welsh football) a great deal that is meanly foul, and much that is brutally foul. The idea among many teams, at any rate with a section in many teams, seems to be to win at any cost. But what pleasure or satisfaction can there be in knowing that you have won or saved a game through foul tactics? We all want to win, but let us play the game winning or losing. To quote a fine saying: 'Any team can win well, but those who know how to lose well show true sportsmanship.'

Let us have vigorous football, but let it be clean. No player should object to being tackled hard if he has the ball, but we want an end of foulness, and we want referees (and captains and committees) who will put it down. Rugby football is a great game, and as long as it is played in the right spirit there is no danger that it will be less popular than it is today. But we must cut out the cancer of foul play.

1. 'You've got to get your first tackle in early, even if it's late.'

Ray Gravell

Obituary

'He was a very powerful forward, who played his hardest bang up to 'no side'. I have never met a man who played more in the spirit of the game. He played one of his greatest games against New Zealand at Cardiff in December 1905. Pritchard was captain of Newport – for whom his first match was in Llewellyn Lloyd's year against Swansea – for three seasons. He was a fine example of what a British sportsman should be and was loved by all who came in contact with him. He was so strong, and yet did not know his own strength. One of his most cherished possessions was a set of jerseys of every International, Colonial and County team he had ever played against, and whenever he got up a team for a charity match he turned them out in these jerseys. He was a fine fisherman and shot. I have heard that in the raid in which he was mortally wounded, I believe by a German officer, Charlie knocked down two of the enemy with his fists. He died as he had lived, playing for his side to the last.'

Major JEC Partridge
(South Africa, Newport and Blackheath)

'Years may come and years may go boys,
But our hearts are still the same
And we know our children's children
Still will play the grand old game

Naughty shall then old friendships sever
Though we drop out from the strife
For in heart and in memory
We are in the team for life'

From the Newport team song, composed by fly half Walter Martin